ITALIAN
VISUAL DICTIONARY

Published by Collins
An imprint of HarperCollins Publishers
Westerhill Road
Bishopbriggs
Glasgow G64 2QT

First Edition 2019

10 9 8 7 6 5 4 3 2

© HarperCollins Publishers 2019

ISBN 978-0-00-829034-4

Collins® is a registered trademark of
HarperCollins Publishers Limited

Typeset by Jouve, India

Printed in China by RR Donnelley APS

Acknowledgements
We would like to thank those authors and
publishers who kindly gave permission for
copyright material to be used in the Collins
Corpus. We would also like to thank Times
Newspapers Ltd for providing valuable data.

A catalogue record for this book is available
from the British Library

If you would like to comment on any aspect
of this book, please contact us at the given
address or online.
E-mail dictionaries@harpercollins.co.uk
 www.facebook.com/collinsdictionary
 @collinsdict

MANAGING EDITOR
Maree Airlie

FOR THE PUBLISHER
Gerry Breslin
Gina Macleod
Kevin Robbins
Robin Scrimgeour

CONTRIBUTORS
Guilia Petito
Lauren Reid
Patrizia Riccardo
Anna Stevenson

TECHNICAL SUPPORT
Claire Dimeo

MIX
Paper from
responsible sources
FSC™ C007454

This book is produced from independently certified FSC™ paper
to ensure responsible forest management.

For more information visit: www.harpercollins.co.uk/green

CONTENTS

4 INTRODUCTION

7 THE ESSENTIALS

17 TRANSPORT

45 IN THE HOME

69 AT THE SHOPS

113 DAY-TO-DAY

141 LEISURE

167 SPORT

191 HEALTH

217 PLANET EARTH

237 CELEBRATIONS AND FESTIVALS

245 INDEX

BAKERY AND PATISSERIE | PANETTERIA E PASTICCERIA

Bread is an essential part of the Italian diet and each region has its own special kinds of bread and rolls. A "panificio" or "panetteria" will sell bread and simple cakes, while for more luxurious cakes you should try a "pasticceria".

YOU MIGHT SAY...

Do you sell...?
Vendete...?

Could I have...?
Posso avere...?

How much are...?
Quanto costano...?

YOU MIGHT HEAR...

Are you being served?
La stanno servendo?

Would you like anything else?
Vuole altro?

I'm sorry, we don't have...
Mi dispiace, non abbiamo...

VOCABULARY

baker il fornaio	loaf la pagnotta	flour la farina
bread il pane	slice la fetta	gluten-free senza glutine
wholemeal bread il pane integrale	crust la crosta	to bake cuocere al forno

YOU SHOULD KNOW...

A range of delicious breakfast pastries is available in many Italian bars, which often also sell sandwiches at lunchtime.

almond biscuits
i biscotti di
mandorle

amaretti biscuits
gli amaretti

bread rolls
i panini

88

4

Whether you're on holiday or staying in Italy for a slightly longer period of time, your **Collins Visual Dictionary** is designed to help you find exactly what you need, when you need it. With over a thousand clear and helpful images, you can quickly locate the vocabulary you are looking for.

The Visual Dictionary includes:

- **10 chapters** arranged thematically, so that you can easily find what you need to suit the situation
- **1** **images** – illustrating essential items
- **2** **YOU MIGHT SAY...** – common phrases that you might want to use
- **3** **YOU MIGHT HEAR...** – common phrases that you might come across
- **4** **VOCABULARY** – common words that you might need
- **5** **YOU SHOULD KNOW...** – tips about local customs or etiquette
- an **index** to find all images quickly and easily
- essential **phrases** and **numbers** listed on the flaps for quick reference

USING YOUR COLLINS VISUAL DICTIONARY

In order to make sure that the phrases and vocabulary in the **Collins Visual Dictionary** are presented in a way that's clear and easy to understand, we have followed certain policies when translating:

1) The polite form "Lei" (you) has been used throughout the text as this is always safe to use, even if a bit formal at times, for example:

How are you? **Come sta?**

Remember that if you are addressing an older person or someone you have just met, you use "Lei". However, if you are speaking to children, or those you know well, you can use "tu". Italian people may invite you to use "tu" with them:

Shall we call each other "tu"? **Diamoci del tu?**

Note that personal pronouns (*I, you* and so on) are not usually used in Italian except for emphasis:

Sto bene. **I'm well.**

2) The grammatical gender of Italian nouns has been indicated using the articles "il" or "lo" (masculine) or "la" (feminine). All nouns which have the article "l'" have been shown with their gender, for example:

year **l'anno** *m*
exit **l'uscita** *f*

In many cases, particularly in words describing professions, the masculine form of the noun tends to be used for both men and women, even if the feminine form exists. In some cases, no feminine form exists at all, for example:

surgeon **il chirurgo**

Where the feminine form is commonly used, it has been shown after the masculine form of the noun:

vet **il veterinario / la veterinaria**

3) In general, the masculine form of adjectives only has been shown for vocabulary items and in phrases, for example:

bored **annoiato**

I'm allergic to... **Sono allergico a...**

However, in some cases both forms are shown:

I'm married. (man) **Sono sposato.**
I'm married. (woman) **Sono sposata.**

Remember that, in Italian, the adjective often changes depending on whether the noun it describes is masculine or feminine. Most masculine adjectives end in "-o" and feminine ones in "-a", so with a feminine noun "contento" becomes "contenta" and "stanco" becomes "stanca". Adjectives ending in "-e" like "felice" remain the same whether the noun they describe is masculine or feminine.

The adjective form also changes if you are talking about a person or object in the singular or in the plural. Usually, the plural form of the adjective is formed by adding "-i" (for masculine nouns) or "-e" (for feminine nouns) to the end of the word. Adjectives ending in "-e" form the plural with "-i":

The girls are bored. **Le ragazze sono annoiate.**
We are happy. **Siamo felici.**

We have created a free audio resource to help you learn and practise the Italian words for all of the images shown in this dictionary. The Italian words in each chapter are spoken by native speakers, giving you the opportunity to listen to each word twice and repeat it yourself. Download the audio from the website below to learn all of the vocabulary you need for communicating in Italian.

www.collinsdictionary.com/resources

Whether you're going to be visiting Italy, or even living there, you'll want to be able to chat with people and get to know them better. Being able to communicate effectively with acquaintances, friends, family, and colleagues is key to becoming more confident in Italian in a variety of everyday situations.

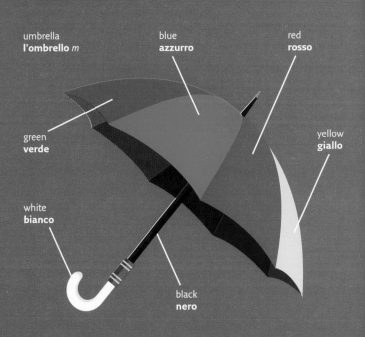

umbrella
l'ombrello *m*

blue
azzurro

red
rosso

green
verde

yellow
giallo

white
bianco

black
nero

Hello.
Ciao.

Good evening.
Buonasera.

See you on Saturday.
A sabato.

Hi!
Ciao!

Good night.
Buonanotte.

Goodbye.
Arrivederci.

Pleased to meet you.
Piacere.

See you soon.
A presto.

Bye!
Ciao!

Good morning/
afternoon.
Buongiorno.

See you tomorrow.
A domani.

Have a good day/
evening!
**Buona giornata /
serata!**

YOU SHOULD KNOW...

Italian people are quite formal when initially introduced, shaking hands upon meeting and parting. Friends and relatives will often greet each other with a kiss on each cheek. "Buongiorno" is used to greet someone during the day, and "Buonasera" in the late afternoon and evening. "Arrivederci" (or if you want to be very polite "Arrivederla") is used when taking your leave. The more informal "Ciao" can be used at all times of the day both when greeting someone and saying goodbye.

Yes.
Si.

Thank you.
Grazie.

I'm sorry.
Mi dispiace.

No.
No.

No, thanks.
No, grazie.

OK!
Va bene!

I don't know.
Non lo so.

Excuse me.
Mi scusi.

You're welcome.
Prego.

Please.
Per favore.

Sorry?
Scusi?

I don't understand.
Non capisco.

Yes, please.
Si, grazie.

How old are you?
Quanti anni ha?

When is your birthday?
Quand'è il suo compleanno?

I'm ... years old.
Ho...

My birthday is on...
Il mio compleanno è...

I was born in...
Sono nato il...

I'm older/younger than...
Sono più grande / giovane di...

Where are you from?
Di dov'è?

Where do you live?
Dove vive?

I'm from...
Vengo da...

...the UK.
il Regno Unito

I live in...
Vivo a...

I'm...
Sono...

Scottish
scozzese

English
inglese

Irish
irlandese

Welsh
gallese

British
britannico

Are you married? (to a man)
È sposato?

Are you married? (to a woman)
È sposata?

Are you single?
È single?

I'm married. (man)
Sono sposato.

I'm married. (woman)
Sono sposata.

I have a partner.
Ho un compagno / una compagna.

I'm single.
Sono single.

I'm divorced. (man)
Sono divorziato.

I'm divorced. (woman)
Sono divorziata.

I'm widowed. (man)
Sono vedovo.

I'm widowed. (woman)
Sono vedova.

Do you have any children?
Ha figli?

I have ... children.
Ho ... figli.

I don't have any children.
Non ho figli.

YOU SHOULD KNOW...

"Signora" and "Signorina" can be translated as "Mrs/Ms" and "Miss" respectively. "Signorina" is less frequently used nowadays and tends to be used for young girls rather than adults; "Signora" can refer to a married or an unmarried woman. It's polite to use someone's title when addressing them or trying to get their attention.

This is my...
**Questo / Questa è
il mio / la mia...**

These are my...
**Questi sono i miei /
le mie...**

husband
il marito

wife
la moglie

boyfriend
il fidanzato

girlfriend
la fidanzata

partner
**il compagno /
la compagna**

fiancé/fiancée
**il fidanzato /
la fidanzata**

son
il figlio

daughter
la figlia

parents
i genitori

father
il padre

mother
la madre

brother
il fratello

sister
la sorella

grandfather
il nonno

grandmother
la nonna

grandson/nephew
il nipote

granddaughter/niece
la nipote

father-in-law
il suocero

mother-in-law
la suocera

daughter-in-law
la nuora

son-in-law
il genero

brother-in-law
il cognato

sister-in-law
la cognata

stepfather
il patrigno

stepmother
la matrigna

stepson
il figliastro

stepdaughter
la figliastra

uncle
lo zio

aunt
la zia

cousin
**il cugino /
la cugina**

extended family
la famiglia allargata

friend
l'amico *m* / **l'amica** *f*

colleague
il / la collega

baby
il bebè

child
**il bambino /
la bambina**

teenager
l'adolescente *m* /
l'adolescente *f*

How are you?
Come sta?

How's it going?
Come va?

How is he/she?
Come sta?

How are they?
Come stanno?

Very well, thanks, and you?
Bene grazie. Lei?

Fine, thanks.
Bene, grazie.

Great!
Benissimo!

So-so.
Così e così.

Not bad, thanks.
Non male, grazie.

Could be worse.
Potrebbe andare peggio.

I'm tired.
Sono stanco.

I'm fine.
Sto bene.

I'm hungry/thirsty.
Ho fame / sete.

I'm full.
Sono pieno.

I'm cold/warm.
Ho freddo / caldo.

I am...
Io sono...

He/She is...
Lui / Lei è...

They are...
Loro sono...

happy
felice

excited
emozionato

calm
calmo

surprised
sorpreso

annoyed
irritato

angry
arrabbiato

sad
triste

worried
preoccupato

afraid
spaventato

bored
annoiato

I feel...
Mi sento...

He/She feels...
Si sente...

They feel...
Si sentono...

well
bene

unwell
malato

better
meglio

worse
peggio

Where do you work?
Dove lavora?

What do you do?
Che fa nella vita?

What's your occupation?
Che lavoro fa?

Do you work/study?
Lavora / Studia?

I'm self-employed.
Sono un lavoratore autonomo.

I'm unemployed.
Sono disoccupato.

I'm at university.
Vado all'università.

I'm retired.
Sono in pensione.

I'm travelling.
Sto viaggiando.

I work from home.
Lavoro da casa.

I work part-/full-time.
Lavoro a tempo parziale / pieno.

I work as a/an...
Lavoro come...

I'm a/an...
Sono un / una...

builder
il costruttore

chef
lo chef

civil servant
**il funzionario pubblico /
la funzionaria pubblica**

cleaner
l'addetto alle pulizie m / **l'addetta alle pulizie** f

dentist
**il dentista /
la dentista**

doctor
il dottore

driver
l'autista m / **l'autista** f

electrician
l'elettricista m

engineer
l'ingegnere m

farmer
**il contadino /
la contadina**

firefighter
il pompiere

fisherman
il pescatore

IT worker
il tecnico informatico

joiner
il falegname

journalist
**il giornalista /
la giornalista**

lawyer
l'avvocato m

mechanic
il meccanico

nurse
l'infermiere m /
l'infermiera f

office worker
l'impiegato m /
l'impiegata f

plumber
l'idraulico m

police officer
**il poliziotto /
la poliziotta**

postal worker
l'impiegato delle poste m /
l'impiegata delle poste f

sailor
il marinaio

salesperson
il venditore /
la venditrice

scientist
lo scienziato /
la scienziata

soldier
il soldato

teacher
il professore /
la professoressa

vet
il veterinario /
la veterinaria

waiter
il cameriere

waitress
la cameriera

I work at/in...
Lavoro a...

business
l'impresa

company
la società

construction site
il cantiere

factory
la fabbrica

government
il governo

hospital
l'ospedale *m*

hotel
l'albergo *m*

office
l'ufficio *m*

restaurant
il ristorante

school
la scuola

shop
il negozio

morning
la mattina

afternoon
il pomeriggio

evening
la sera

night
la notte

midday
il mezzogiorno

midnight
la mezzanotte

What time is it?
Che ora è?

It's nine o'clock.
Sono le nove.

It's ten past nine.
Sono le nove e dieci.

It's quarter past nine.
**Sono le nove
e un quarto.**

It's 25 past nine.
**Sono le nove
e venticinque.**

It's half past nine.
**Sono le nove
e mezza.**

It's 20 to ten.
**Sono le dieci meno
venti.**

It's quarter to ten.
**Sono le dieci meno
un quarto.**

It's five to ten.
**Sono le dieci meno
cinque.**

It's 10 a.m.
**Sono le dieci
di mattina.**

It's 5 p.m.
**Sono le cinque di
pomeriggio.**

It's 17:30.
**Sono le diciassette
e trenta.**

When...?
Quando...?

... in 60 seconds/
two minutes.
**... tra 60 secondi /
due minuti.**

... in an hour.
... tra un'ora.

... in quarter of an hour.
... tra un quarto d'ora.

... in half an hour.
... tra mezz'ora.

today
oggi

tonight
stasera

tomorrow
domani

yesterday
ieri

the day after tomorrow
dopodomani

the day before yesterday
l'altro ieri

early
in anticipo / presto

late
tardi

soon
presto

later
più tardi

now
ora

YOU SHOULD KNOW...

In Italy it's more common to use the 24-hour clock. Note that you use "sono",
except when talking about midday, midnight and one o'clock, when you use "è".

| Monday lunedì | Wednesday mercoledì | Friday venerdì | Sunday domenica |
| Tuesday martedì | Thursday giovedì | Saturday sabato | |

January gennaio	April aprile	July luglio	October ottobre
February febbraio	May maggio	August agosto	November novembre
March marzo	June giugno	September settembre	December dicembre

day il giorno	weekly settimanale	in February a febbraio
weekend il fine settimana	fortnightly bimensile	in 2018 nel 2018
week la settimana	monthly mensile	in the '80s negli anni '80
fortnight due settimane	yearly annuale	spring la primavera
quarter il trimestre	on Mondays di lunedì	summer l'estate f
month il mese	every Sunday ogni domenica	autumn l'autunno m
year l'anno m	last Thursday giovedì scorso	winter l'inverno m
decade il decennio	next Friday venerdì prossimo	in spring/winter in primavera / inverno
daily giornaliero	the week before/after la settimana prima / dopo	

How's the weather?
Che tempo fa?

What's the forecast for today/tomorrow?
Quali sono le previsioni metereologiche per oggi / domani?

How warm/cold is it?
Quanto è caldo / freddo?

Is it going to rain?
Sta per piovere?

What a lovely day!
Che bella giornata!

What awful weather!
Che brutto tempo!

It's raining/windy/foggy.
È piovoso / ventoso / nebbioso.

It's sunny.
C'è il sole.

It's cloudy.
È nuvoloso.

It's misty.
C'è foschia.

It's freezing.
C'è il gelo.

It's snowing.
Nevica.

It's stormy.
C'è la bufera.

It's changeable.
È mutevole.

It is...
È...

nice
bello

horrible
brutto

hot
caldo

warm
tiepido

cool
fresco

wet
bagnato

humid
umido

mild
mite

temperature
la temperatura

sun
il sole

rain
la pioggia

snow
la neve

hail
la grandine

ice
il ghiaccio

wind
il vento

gale
il vento forte

mist
la foschia

fog
la nebbia

thunder
il tuono

lightning
il fulmine

thunderstorm
il temporale

cloud
la nuvola

TRANSPORT | MEZZI DI TRASPORTO

Travelling to and around Italy has never been easier. You can travel to Italy from the UK by air, rail (via France), or road. Italy's extensive railway system boasts some of the fastest passenger trains in the world – it can be quicker to travel by train than by plane between certain cities – and the country is well connected by road. Local public transport is cheap and widely developed, with some cities having underground systems as well as trams and buses.

helicopter
l'elicottero *m*

rotor
il rotore

blade
la pala

cockpit
**la cabina
di pilotaggio**

nose
la prua

tail
la coda

When asking for directions, it's easiest simply to state your destination, followed by "per favore".

YOU MIGHT SAY...

Excuse me...
Mi scusi...

Where is...?
Dov'è...?

Which way is...?
In che direzione è...?

What's the quickest way to...?
Qual'è la via più diretta per...

How far away is it?
Quanto dista?

Is it far from here?
È lontano?

I'm lost.
Mi sono perso.

I'm looking for...
Sto cercando...

I'm going...
Sto andando...

Can I walk there?
Posso andare a piedi?

YOU MIGHT HEAR...

It's over there.
È laggiù.

It's in the other direction.
È nella direzione opposta.

It's ... metres/minutes from here.
È a ... metri / minuti di distanza da qui.

Go straight ahead.
Vada dritto.

Turn left/right.
Giri a sinistra / destra.

Turn right.
Giri a destra.

It's next to...
È accanto a...

It's opposite ...
È difronte a...

It's near to...
È vicino a...

Follow the signs for...
Segua le indicazioni per...

street **la strada**	rush hour **l'ora di punta** *f*	to walk **camminare**
commuter **il pendolare**	public transport **il trasporto pubblico**	to drive **guidare**
driver **l'autista** *m* / **l'autista** *f*	taxi **il taxi**	to return **ritornare**
passenger **il passeggero**	taxi rank **la stazione dei taxi**	to cross **attraversare**
pedestrian **il pedone**	road sign **la segnaletica stradale**	to turn **girare**
traffic **il traffico**	directions **le direzioni stradali**	to commute **fare il pendolare**
traffic jam **l'ingorgo stradale** *m*	route **l'itinerario** *m*	to take a taxi **prendere un taxi**

map
la mappa

ticket
il biglietto

timetable
l'orario *m*

Traffic drives on the right-hand side in Italy – at intersections, vehicles must give way to drivers approaching from their right. Remember to carry your driving licence, proof of insurance, ID, and car registration documents with you while driving in Italy.

YOU MIGHT SAY...

Is this the road to...?
È questa la strada per...?

Can I park here?
Posso parcheggiare qui?

Do I have to pay to park?
Il parcheggio è a pagamento?

Where can I hire a car?
Dove posso affittare una macchina?

I'd like to hire a car...
Vorrei affittare una macchina.

... for four days/a week.
... per quattro giorni / una settimana.

What is your daily/weekly rate?
Qual è la vostra tariffa giornaliera / settimanale?

When/Where must I return it?
Quando / Dove la riporto?

Where is the nearest petrol station?
Dov'è la stazione di servizio più vicina?

I'd like ... litres/euros of fuel, please.
Vorrei ... litri / euro di benzina, per favore.

YOU MIGHT HEAR...

You can/can't park here.
Può / Non può parcheggiare qui.

It's free to park here.
Il parcheggio qui è gratuito.

It costs ... to park here.
Parcheggiare qui costa...

Car hire is ... per day/week.
L'affitto della macchina costa ... al giorno / alla settimana.

May I see your documents, please?
Posso vedere i suoi docimenti, per favore?

Please return it to...
La riporti a ..., per favore.

Please return the car with a full tank of fuel.
Riporti la macchina con il serbatoio pieno, per favore.

Which pump are you at?
A quale pompa è?

How much fuel would you like?
Quanta benzina?

people carrier **il monovolume**	hybrid (car) **la (macchina) ibrida**	gearbox **il cambio**
caravan **il caravan**	engine **il motore**	transmission **la trasmissione**
motorhome **il camper**	battery **la batteria**	Breathalyser® **l'etilometro** *m*
passenger seat **il sedile passeggero**	brake **i freni**	to start the engine **accendere il motore**
driver's seat **il posto di guida**	accelerator **l'acceleratore** *m*	to brake **frenare**
back seat **il sedile posteriore**	air conditioning **l'aria condizionata** *f*	to overtake **sorpassare**
child seat **il seggiolino per bambini**	clutch **la frizione**	to park **parcheggiare**
roof rack **il portapacchi**	cruise control **la regolazione automatica della velocità**	to reverse **fare retromarcia**
sunroof **il tettuccio apribile**	exhaust (pipe) **il tubo di scappamento**	to slow down **rallentare**
automatic (car) **la (macchina) automatica**		to speed up **accelerare**
electric (car) **la (macchina) elettrica**	fuel tank **il serbatoio del carburante**	to stop **fermarsi**

YOU SHOULD KNOW...

In Italy it is illegal to drive with devices that can detect radars and speed cameras, but this restriction does not apply to the radar detection built into sat-navs.

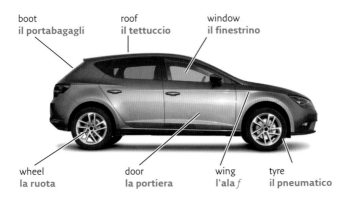

boot
il portabagagli

roof
il tettuccio

window
il finestrino

wheel
la ruota

door
la portiera

wing
l'ala *f*

tyre
il pneumatico

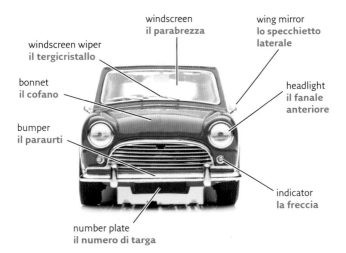

windscreen
il parabrezza

wing mirror
lo specchietto laterale

windscreen wiper
il tergicristallo

bonnet
il cofano

headlight
il fanale anteriore

bumper
il paraurti

indicator
la freccia

number plate
il numero di targa

dashboard
il cruscotto

fuel gauge
**l'indicatore del
carburante** *m*

gearstick
il cambio

glove compartment
il vano portaoggetti

handbrake
il freno a mano

headrest
il poggiatesta

ignition
l'accensione *f*

rearview mirror
**lo specchietto
retrovisore**

sat nav
il navigatore

seatbelt
**la cintura di
sicurezza**

speedometer
il tachimetro

steering wheel
il volante

Italy has an excellent motorway system, but be aware that almost all the "autostrade" are toll-paying. Dipped headlights must be used at all times outside built-up areas and in all tunnels.

VOCABULARY

single-track road
la strada a una sola corsia

corner
la curva

exit
l'uscita *f*

slip road
la rampa d'accesso

layby
la piazzola di sosta

speed limit
il limite di velocità

diversion
la deviazione stradale

driving licence
la patente

car registration document
il documento di immatricolazione della macchina

car insurance
l'assicurazione stradale *f*

car hire/rental
l'autonoleggio *m*

unleaded petrol
la benzina senza piombo

diesel
il diesel

roadworks
i lavori stradali

YOU SHOULD KNOW...

Speed limits on Italian roads go by kmph, not mph. The limits are 50 kmph in built-up areas, 70 kmph on some urban motorways, 90 kmph on secondary roads, 110 kmph on main roads, and 130 kmph on motorways (sometimes increased to 150 kmph on three-lane motorways).

accessible parking space
il parcheggio accessibile

bridge
il ponte

car park
il parcheggio

car wash
l'autolavaggio *m*

fuel pump
la pompa di benzina

junction
il bivio

kerb
il cordolo

lane
la corsia

level crossing
il passaggio a livello

motorway
l'autostrada *f*

parking meter
il parchimetro

parking space
il parcheggio

pavement
il marciapiede

petrol station
il benzinaio

pothole
la buca

road
la strada

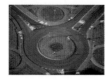

roundabout
la rotonda

speed camera
l'autovelox *m*

traffic cone
il cono di traffico

toll point
il casello autostradale

traffic lights
il semaforo

traffic warden
l'ausiliare del traffico *m* / **l'ausiliare del traffico** *f*

tunnel
il tunnel

zebra crossing
le strisce pedonali

CAR TROUBLE | PROBLEMI CON LA MACCHINA

If you break down on the motorway, put on your hi-viz vest, install the warning triangle, then call the police or the breakdown service operating in that area, using one of the emergency telephones that are located every 2 km along the side of the road. Otherwise, call 112 to contact the emergency services.

YOU MIGHT SAY...

Can you help me?
Può aiutarmi?

I've broken down.
Sono in panne.

I've had an accident.
Ho avuto un incidente.

I've run out of petrol.
È finita la benzina.

I've got a flat tyre.
Mi si è bucata una ruota.

I've lost my car keys.
Ho perso le chiavi della macchina.

The car won't start.
La macchina non parte.

There's a problem with...
C'è un problema con...

I've been injured.
Sono ferito.

Call an ambulance/the police!
Chiami un'ambulanza / la polizia!

Can you send a breakdown van?
Può mandare un carro attrezzi?

Is there a garage/petrol station nearby?
C'è un garage / una stazione di servizio nelle vicinanze?

Can you tow me to a garage?
Può portarmi a rimorchio da un meccanico?

Can you help me change this wheel?
Può aiutarmi a cambiare una ruota?

How much will a repair cost?
Quanto costa una riparazione?

When will the car be fixed?
Quando sarà pronta la macchina?

May I take your insurance details?
Posso avere i suoi dati assicurativi?

Do you need any help?
Posso aiutarla?

Are you hurt?
Si è fatto male?

What's wrong with your car?
Cosa c'è che non va con la macchina?

Where have you broken down?
Dove è andato in panne?

I can tow you to...
Posso portarla a rimorchio a...

I can give you a jumpstart.
Posso aiutarla a far ripartire la macchina con i cavi.

The repairs will cost...
La riparazione costa...

We need to order new parts.
Dobbiamo ordinare le parti.

The car will be ready by...
La macchina sarà pronta per...

I need your insurance details.
Ho bisogno dei dati assicurativi.

VOCABULARY

accident
l'incidente *m*

breakdown
il guasto

collision
la collisione

flat tyre
la ruota bucata

to break down
avere un guasto

to have an accident
avere un incidente

to have a flat tyre
avere una ruota bucata

to change a tyre
cambiare la ruota

to tow
trascinare a rimorchio

YOU SHOULD KNOW...

When driving in Italy, you are legally required to have the following in your car: your driver's licence and car registration; proof of ID and insurance; spare tyre; warning triangle; hi-viz vests; and headlamp beam deflectors.

airbag
l'airbag *m*

antifreeze
l'antigelo *m*

emergency phone
il telefono
d'emergenza

garage
l'autofficina *f*

hi-viz vest
il giubbotto ad alta
visibilità

jack
il martinetto

jump leads
i cavi di avviamento

mechanic
il meccanico

snow chains
le catene da neve

spare wheel
la ruota di scorta

tow truck
il carro attrezzi

warning triangle
il triangolo di
segnalazione

Local bus or tram services are often well organized and useful; many mountain areas in Italy are served by coaches.

YOU MIGHT SAY...

Is there a bus to...?
C'è un autobus per...?

When is the next bus to...?
Quand'è il prossimo autobus per...?

Which bus goes to the city centre?
Quale autobus va al centro?

Where is the bus stop?
Dov'è la fermata dell'autobus?

Which stand does the coach leave from?
Da quale fermata parte il pullman?

Where can I buy tickets?
Dove posso comprare i biglietti?

How much is it to go to...?
Quant'è il biglietto per...?

A full/half fare, please.
Un biglietto a prezzo pieno / metà prezzo, per favore.

A single/return ticket, please.
Un biglietto di andata / di andata e ritorno, per favore.

Could you tell me when to get off?
Può dirmi dove scendere?

How many stops is it?
Quante fermate sono?

YOU MIGHT HEAR...

The number 17 goes to...
Il numero 17 va...

The bus stop is down the road.
La fermata dell'autobus è in fondo alla strada.

It leaves from stand 21.
Parte dalla fermata 21.

There's a bus every 10 minutes.
C'è un autobus ogni 10 minuti.

You buy tickets at the machine/office.
Può comprare i biglietti ai distributori automatici / alla biglietteria.

This is your stop, sir/madam.
Questa è la sua fermata, signore / signora.

bus route	bus pass	wheelchair access
l'itinerario degli autobus *m*	l'abbonamento dell'autobus *m*	l'accesso per sedia a rotelle *m*
bus lane	fare	shuttle bus
la corsia preferenziale	la tariffa	l'autobus navetta *m*
bus stop	full/half fare	school bus
la fermata dell'autobus	il biglietto a prezzo pieno / a metà prezzo	lo scuolabus
bus station	concession	tour bus
la stazione degli autobus	il biglietto agevolato	l'autobus turistico *m*
		to catch the bus
		prendere l'autobus

YOU SHOULD KNOW...

Bus and tram tickets can be bought from ticket machines, newspaper kiosks, tobacconists, and bars. You must validate ("timbrare" or "obliterare") your ticket on the bus or tram at the start of your journey.

bus
l'autobus *m*

bus shelter
la fermata
dell'autobus

coach
il pullman

minibus
il minibus

tram
il tram

trolley bus
il filobus

31

Italy has many long-distance cycle routes, but there is no national cycle network. Most traffic-free cycleways are in the north of the country.

YOU MIGHT SAY...

Where can I hire a bicycle?
Dove posso affittare una bicicletta?

How much is it to hire a bicycle?
Quanto costa affittare una bicicletta?

My bike has a puncture.
La ruota della bicicletta è bucata.

Is there a cycle path nearby?
C'è una pista ciclabile qui vicino?

YOU MIGHT HEAR...

You must wear a helmet.
Deve mettere un casco.

There's a cycle path from ... to...
C'è una pista ciclabile da ... a...

VOCABULARY

cyclist **il / la ciclista**	bike rack **la rastrelliera per bici**	cycling shorts **i pantaloncini da ciclismo**
mountain bike **la mountain bike**	child seat **il seggiolino per bambini**	to get a puncture **bucare**
road bike **la bicicletta da strada**	cycle lane **la pista ciclabile**	to cycle **pedalare**
bike stand **il cavalletto**	puncture repair kit **il kit di riparazione per le forature**	to go for a bike ride **andare a fare un giro in bicicletta**

YOU SHOULD KNOW...

Italy hosts the world-famous road race, the Giro d'Italia.

bell
il campanello

bike lock
il lucchetto per bici

front light
la luce anteriore

helmet
il casco

pump
la pompa per bicicletta

reflector
il catarifrangente

BICYCLE

handlebars
il manubrio

gears
le marce

crossbar
il tubo orizzontale

saddle
il sellino

frame
il telaio

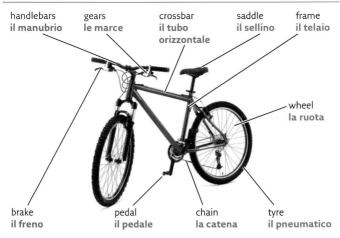

wheel
la ruota

brake
il freno

pedal
il pedale

chain
la catena

tyre
il pneumatico

VOCABULARY

motorcyclist **il / la motociclista**	fuel tank **il serbatoio del carburante**	mudguard **il parafango**
moped **il motorino**	handlebars **il manubrio**	exhaust pipe **il tubo di scappamento**
scooter **lo scooter**	headlight **il fanale anteriore**	kickstand **il cavalletto**

YOU SHOULD KNOW...

The scooter has become a symbol of Italy, with Italians legally allowed to ride one from the age of 14. Motorcyclists must wear helmets and drive with their lights on.

boots
gli stivali

crash helmet
il casco protettivo

helmet cam
la videocamera da casco

leather gloves
i guanti di pelle

leather jacket
la giacca di pelle

motorbike
la moto

Italy has a well-developed, well-organized national railway system. Before boarding a local or regional train, it's important to validate ("obliterare") your ticket: failure to do so can result in a fine. However, you don't need to validate your ticket on trains you have booked as your ticket will be valid for that train only.

YOU MIGHT SAY...

Is there a train to...?
C'è un treno per...?

When is the next train to...?
Quand'è il prossimo treno per...?

Where is the nearest metro station?
Dov'è la stazione metro più vicina?

Which platform does it leave from?
Da quale binario parte?

Which line do I take for...?
Che linea prendo per...

A ticket to ..., please.
Un biglietto per ..., per favore.

A return ticket to ..., please.
Un biglietto andata e ritorno per ..., per favore.

I'd like to reserve a seat/couchette, please.
Vorrei prenotare un posto / una cuccetta, per favore.

Do I have to change train?
Devo cambiare treno?

Where do I change for...?
Dove cambio per...?

Where is platform 4?
Dov'è il binario numero 4?

Is this the right platform for...?
Questo e' il binario giusto per...?

Is this the train for...?
È questo il treno per...?

Is this seat free?
È libero questo posto?

Where is the restaurant car?
Dov'è il vagone ristorante?

I've missed my train!
Ho perso il treno!

YOU SHOULD KNOW...

There are underground ("metropolitana") systems in several Italian cities including Rome, Naples and Milan, with the one in Milan being the most extensive.

The next train leaves at...
Il prossimo treno parte alle...

Yes, this is the right platform.
Sì, questo è il binario giusto.

Would you like a single or return ticket?
Vuole un biglietto di sola andata o di andata e ritorno?

No, you have to go to platform 2.
No, deve andare al binario numero 2.

I'm sorry, this journey is fully booked.
Mi dispiace, non ci sono più biglietti.

This seat is free/taken.
Questo posto è libero / occupato.

The restaurant car is in coach D.
Il vagone ristorante è la carrozza D.

You must change at...
Deve cambiare treno a...

The next stop is...
La prossima fermata è...

Platform 4 is down there.
Il binario numero 4 è laggiù.

Change here for...
Scendere qui per...

VOCABULARY

rail network **la rete ferroviaria**	metro station **la stazione di metropolitana**	e-ticket **il biglietto elettronico**
high-speed train **il treno ad alta velocità**	left luggage **il deposito bagagli**	first-class **di prima classe**
passenger train **il treno passeggeri**	railcard **l'abbonamento ferroviario** *m*	quiet coach **la carrozza silenziosa**
freight train **il treno merci**	single ticket **il biglietto di sola andata**	seat reservation **il posto prenotato**
sleeper **il vagone letto**		to change trains **cambiare treno**
line **la linea**	return ticket **il biglietto di andata e ritorno**	to validate a ticket **obliterare un biglietto**

carriage
la carrozza

couchette
la cuccetta

departure board
il tabellone delle partenze

guard
la guardia

light railway
la metropolitana leggera

locomotive
la locomotiva

luggage rack
il ripiano portabagagli

metro
la metropolitana

platform
il binario

porter
il facchino

restaurant car
il vagone ristorante

refreshments trolley
il carrello

signal box
la cabina di manovra

sliding doors
le porte scorrevoli

ticket barrier
il tornello

ticket machine
**la biglietteria
automatica**

ticket office
la biglietteria

track
il binario

train station
**la stazione
ferroviaria**

train
il treno

validation machine
l'obliteratrice *f*

Italy has many airports, but many airlines only operate seasonal routes to and from the UK, so check when flights to less central destinations are available.

YOU MIGHT SAY...

I'm looking for check-in/my gate.
**Sto cercando il check-in /
il mio gate d'imbarco.**

I'm checking in one case.
Ho una valigia da mettere in stiva.

Which gate does the plane
leave from?
Da che gate parte l'aereo?

When does the gate open/close?
Quando apre / chiude il gate?

Is the flight on time?
È in orario il volo?

I'd like a window/aisle seat, please.
**Vorrei un posto vicino al
finestrino / lungo il corridoio,
per favore.**

I've lost my luggage.
Ho perso il bagaglio.

My flight has been delayed.
Il mio volo è in ritardo.

I've missed my flight/connection.
**Ho perso il volo /
la coincidenza.**

Is there a shuttle bus service?
C'è un servizio di navetta?

YOU MIGHT HEAR...

Check-in has opened for flight...
Il check-in è aperto per il volo...

May I see your ticket/passport,
please?
**Posso avere il suo biglietto /
passaporto, per favore?**

How many bags are you checking in?
Quante valigie in stiva?

Your luggage exceeds the
maximum weight.
**Il suo bagaglio eccede il peso
massimo.**

Please go to gate number...
**Per favore, vada al gate
numero...**

Your flight is on time/delayed/
cancelled.
**Il suo volo è in orario /
in ritardo / cancellato.**

Is this your bag?
È questo il suo bagaglio?

Flight ... is now ready for boarding.
Il volo ... è pronto per l'imbarco.

Last call for passenger...
**L'ultima chiamata per il
passeggero...**

aeroplane
l'aeroplano m

wing
l'ala f

fuselage
la fusoliera

engine
il motore

airline
la linea aerea

terminal
il terminal

Arrivals/Departures
gli arrivi /
le partenze

security
il controllo di
sicurezza

passport control
il controllo
passaporti

customs
la dogana

cabin crew
l'equipaggio m

business class
la business class

economy class
l'economy class f

aisle
il corridoio

tray table
il tavolino

overhead locker
la cappelliera

seatbelt
la cintura di sicurezza

hold
la stiva

hold luggage
il bagaglio che ha
passato il controllo
di sicurezza

excess baggage
il bagaglio in
eccesso

hand/cabin baggage
il bagaglio a mano

connecting flight
la coincidenza

jetlag
il jetlag

to check in (online)
effettuare il check-
in (online)

aeroplane
l'aeroplano m

airport
l'aeroporto m

baggage reclaim
il ritiro bagagli

boarding card
la carta d'imbarco

cabin
la cabina

check-in desk
il check-in

cockpit
la cabina di pilotaggio

departure board
il tabellone delle partenze

duty-free shop
il duty free

holdall
la borsa da viaggio

luggage trolley
il carrello portabagagli

passport
il passaporto

pilot
il pilota / la pilota

runway
la pista

suitcase
la valigia

There are numerous ferry ports along the coasts of Italy, connecting to different parts of the country including the many islands, as well as to other Mediterranean countries such as Spain and Greece.

YOU MIGHT SAY...

When is the next boat to...?
Quand'è il prossimo battello per...?

Where does the boat leave from?
Da dove parte il battello?

What time is the last boat to...?
A che ora è l'ultimo battello per...?

How long is the trip/crossing?
Quanto dura il viaggio / la traversata?

How many crossings a day are there?
Quante traversate ci sono al giorno?

How much for ... passengers?
Quant'è per ... passeggeri?

How much is it for a vehicle?
Quanto costa il biglietto con la macchina?

I feel seasick.
Ho il mal di mare.

YOU MIGHT HEAR...

The boat leaves from...
Il battello parte da...

The trip/crossing lasts...
Il viaggio / La traversata dura...

There are ... crossings a day.
Ci sono ... traversate al giorno.

The ferry is delayed/cancelled.
Il traghetto è in ritardo / cancellato.

Sea conditions are good/bad.
Le condizioni marittime sono buone / cattive.

VOCABULARY

ferry crossing
la traversata in traghetto

ferry terminal
il terminal dei traghetti

car deck
il ponte garage

| deck | funnel | captain |
| il ponte | il fumaiolo | il capitano |

lifeboat	pier	crew
la scialuppa di	il pontile	l'equipaggio *m*
salvataggio		

	port	to board
stern	il porto	salire a bordo di
la poppa		

	canal	to sail
bow	il canale	navigare
la prua		

	lock	to dock
porthole	la chiusa	entrare in porto
l'oblò *m*		

| | coastguard | |
| | la guardia costiera | |

GENERAL

anchor
l'ancora *f*

buoy
la boa

gangway
la passerella

harbour
il porto

jetty
il molo

lifebuoy
il salvagente

lifejacket
il giubbotto di salvataggio

marina
il porticciolo

mooring
l'ormeggio *m*

BOATS

canal boat
la chiatta

canoe
la canoa

ferry
il traghetto

inflatable dinghy
il canotto

kayak
il kayak

liner
il transatlantico

rowing boat
la barca a remi

sailing boat
la barca a vela

yacht
lo yacht

IN THE HOME | A CASA

Italy attracts huge numbers of tourists and expats looking for a place to call home for a time, whether it's for a holiday or a longer-term stay. This could be a central city apartment, a cosy farmhouse in a rural spot, or an expansive and luxurious villa.

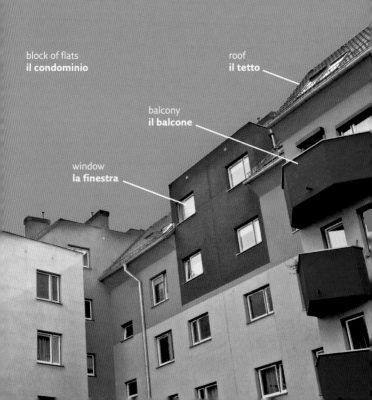

block of flats
il condominio

roof
il tetto

balcony
il balcone

window
la finestra

Most of Italy's population lives in urban areas, although it's quite common for people to head out of the city for "un fine settimana al mare" (a weekend at the seaside) or "in campagna" (in the country).

YOU MIGHT SAY...

I live in...
Vivo a...

I'm staying at...
Sto a / alloggio presso...

My address is...
Il mio indirizzo è...

I have a flat/house.
Ho un appartamento / una casa.

I'm the homeowner/tenant.
Sono il proprietario / l'affittuario.

I've recently moved.
Mi sono trasferito da poco.

I'm moving to...
Mi sto trasferendo a...

I don't like this area.
Questa zona non mi piace.

I'd like to buy/rent a property here.
Vorrei comprare / affittare una proprietà qui.

YOU MIGHT HEAR...

Where do you live?
Dove vive?

Where are you staying?
Dove alloggia?

How long have you lived here?
Da quanto tempo vive qui?

What's your address, please?
Mi da il suo indirizzo, per favore?

Are you the owner/tenant?
Lei è il propriatario / l'affittuario?

Do you like this area?
Le piace questa zona?

Where are you moving to?
Dove si trasferisce?

YOU SHOULD KNOW...

A property that is furnished ("ammobiliato") will cost around 20% more than one that is unfurnished ("vuoto"), but otherwise the rental agreements are the same. The protection available for tenants in Italy is good, but make sure you understand what your rights are if you intend to rent long term.

VOCABULARY

villa **la villa**	estate agent **l'agente immobiliare** *m*	rent **l'affitto** *m*
townhouse **la casa in città**	landlord **il proprietario**	holiday let **la casa vacanza**
building **il palazzo**	landlady **la proprietaria**	to rent **affittare**
address **l'indirizzo** *m*	tenant **l'affittuario** *m*	to own **possedere**
suburb **il sobborgo**	neighbour **il vicino di casa / la vicina di casa**	to live **vivere**
district **il quartiere**	mortgage **il mutuo**	to move house **cambiare casa** to build a house **costruire una casa**

TYPES OF BUILDING

apartment block
il condominio

bungalow
il bungalow

detached house
il villino

farmhouse
la fattoria

semi-detached house
la casa bifamiliare

studio flat
il monolocale

YOU MIGHT SAY...

We are renovating our home.
Stiamo ristrutturando casa.

There's no hot water.
Non c'è acqua calda.

We are redecorating the lounge.
Stiamo ridipingendo il salotto.

We have a power cut.
Abbiamo un blackout.

There's a problem with...
C'è un problema con...

I need a plumber/an electrician.
Ho bisogno di un indraulico /
elettricista.

It's not working.
Non funziona.

Can you recommend anyone?
Può consigliare qualcuno?

The drains are blocked.
Gli scarichi sono intasati.

Can it be repaired?
Si può riparare?

The boiler has broken.
La caldaia si è rotta.

I can smell gas/smoke.
Sento odore di gas / fumo.

YOU MIGHT HEAR...

What seems to be the problem?
Quale potrebbe essere il
problema?

Where is the meter/fusebox?
Dov'è il contatore / il quadro
elettrico?

How long has it been broken/
leaking?
Da quanto tempo è rotto /
perde acqua?

Here's a number for a plumber/
an electrician.
Questo è il numero di un
idraulico / elettricista.

VOCABULARY

room la stanza	attic la mansarda	wall il muro
cellar la cantina	ceiling il soffitto	floor il pavimento

battery	central heating	balcony
la batteria	il riscaldamento	il balcone
	centralizzato	
plug		skylight
la spina	satellite dish	il lucernario
	l'antenna	
adaptor	parabolica *f*	power cut
l'adattatore *m*		il blackout
	porch	
socket	il portico	to fix
la presa		riparare
	back door	
electricity	la porta sul retro	to decorate
l'elettricità *f*		dipingere
	French windows	
air conditioning	la porta finestra	to renovate
l'aria condizionata *f*		ristrutturare

Tradespeople in Italy must comply with all local and national regulations.

INSIDE

boiler	ceiling fan	extension cable
la caldaia	il ventilatore da	la prolunga
	soffitto	

fusebox	heater	light bulb
il quadro elettrico	la stufa	la lampadina

meter
il contatore

radiator
il termosifone

security alarm
l'allarme di
sicurezza *m*

smoke alarm
il rilevatore di fumo

thermostat
il termostato

wood-burning stove
la stufa a legna

OUTSIDE

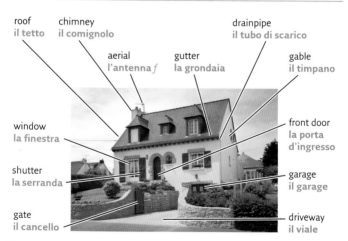

roof
il tetto

chimney
il comignolo

aerial
l'antenna *f*

gutter
la grondaia

drainpipe
il tubo di scarico

gable
il timpano

window
la finestra

front door
la porta
d'ingresso

shutter
la serranda

garage
il garage

gate
il cancello

driveway
il viale

YOU MIGHT SAY/HEAR...

Would you like to come round?
Vuoi venire a casa mia?

Shall I take my shoes off?
Mi tolgo le scarpe?

Hi! Come in.
Ciao! Entra pure.

Can I use your bathroom?
Posso usare il bagno?

Make yourself at home.
Fai come se fossi a casa tua.

Thanks for inviting me over.
Grazie per l'invito.

VOCABULARY

doorway **l'entrata** *f*	stairwell **la tromba delle scale**	key **la chiave**
corridor **il corridoio**	staircase **la scala**	to buzz somebody in **far entrare qualcuno**
hallway **l'ingresso** *m*	lift **l'ascensore** *m*	to wipe one's feet **pulirsi le scarpe**
landing **il pianerottolo**	doormat **lo zerbino**	to hang one's jacket up **appendere la giacca**

doorbell
il campanello

intercom
il citofono

letterbox
la cassetta della posta

VOCABULARY

carpet
il tappeto

floorboard
l'asse del pavimento *f*

suite
la suite

sofa bed
il divano letto

table lamp
la lampada da tavolo

home entertainment system
l'home theater *m*

cable TV
la televisione via cavo

satellite TV
la televisione satellitare

smart TV
la smart TV

TV on demand
la TV on demand

to relax
rilassarsi

to sit down
sedersi

to watch TV
guardare la televisione

GENERAL

bookcase
la libreria

curtains
le tende

display cabinet
l'armadio espositivo *m*

DVD/Blu-ray® player
il lettore DVD / Blu-ray®

radio
la radio

remote control
il telecomando

sideboard
la credenza

TV stand
il porta TV

Venetian blind
la tenda veneziana

LOUNGE

fireplace
il camino

coffee table
il tavolino

picture
il quadro

wall light
la luce a muro

TV
il televisore

sofa
il divano

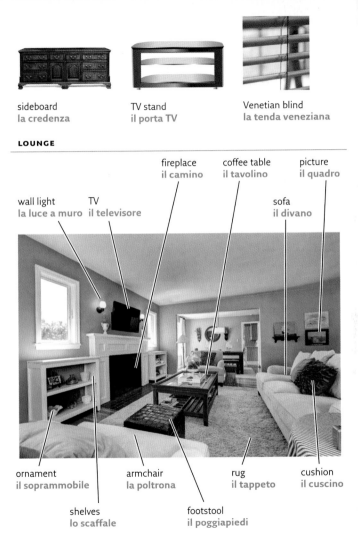

ornament
il soprammobile

armchair
la poltrona

rug
il tappeto

cushion
il cuscino

shelves
lo scaffale

footstool
il poggiapiedi

In the past, kitchens in Italy were not usually treated as entertaining spaces, but with more informal modern lifestyles, open-plan kitchens have become more common.

VOCABULARY

electric cooker
il fornello elettrico

kettle
il bollitore

to clean the worktops
pulire il ripiano della cucina

gas cooker
il fornello a gas

to cook
cucinare

to put away the groceries
sistemare la spesa

cooker hood
la cappa

to wash up
lavare i piatti

MISCELLANEOUS ITEMS

aluminium foil
la carta d'alluminio

bin bag
il sacco della spazzatura

bread bin
il portapane

clingfilm
la pellicola

kitchen roll
la carta da cucina

pedal bin
la pattumiera a pedale

baking tray
la teglia

cafetière
la caffettiera

casserole dish
la casseruola

chopping board
il tagliere

coffee pot
la macchina da caffè

colander
lo scolapasta

corkscrew
il cavatappi

food processor
il frullatore

frying pan
la padella

grater
la grattugia

hand mixer
il frullatore

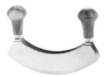

herb chopper
la mezzaluna

ladle
il mestolo

masher
lo schiacciapatate

measuring jug
il recipiente
graduato

mixing bowl
la scodella

pasta machine
la macchina per la
pasta

peeler
il pelapatate

rolling pin
il mattarello

saucepan
la pentola

sieve
il colino

spatula
la spatola

tin opener
l'apriscatole m

toaster
il tostapane

whisk
la frusta

wok
il wok

wooden spoon
il cucchiaio di legno

THE KITCHEN

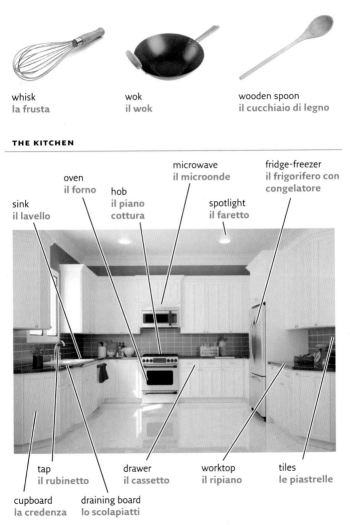

sink
il lavello

oven
il forno

hob
il piano cottura

microwave
il microonde

fridge-freezer
il frigorifero con congelatore

spotlight
il faretto

tap
il rubinetto

drawer
il cassetto

worktop
il ripiano

tiles
le piastrelle

cupboard
la credenza

draining board
lo scolapiatti

VOCABULARY

dining table **la tavola**	crockery **le stoviglie**	to set the table **apparecchiare**
place mat **la tovaglietta**	cutlery **le posate**	to dine **cenare**
coaster **il sottobicchiere**	glassware **la cristalleria**	to clear the table **sparecchiare**

YOU SHOULD KNOW...

When dining in an Italian home, make sure you arrive slightly after the suggested time, never before. You should not begin eating until the host or the most senior person there has started eating.

GENERAL

gravy boat
la salsiera

napkin
il tovagliolo

pepper mill
il macinapepe

salad bowl
l'insalatiera *f*

salt cellar
la saliera

serving dish
il piatto da portata

bowl
l'insalatiera *f*

champagne flute
il flute da spumante

cup and saucer
la tazza e il piattino

knife and fork
il coltello e la
forchetta

plate
il piatto

spoon
il cucchiaio

teaspoon
il cucchiaino

tumbler
il bicchiere

wine glass
il calice da vino

VOCABULARY

single bed
il letto singolo

double bed
il letto matrimoniale

master bedroom
la camera da letto

spare bedroom
la camera degli ospiti

en-suite bathroom
il bagno privato

nursery
la stanza dei bambini

bedding
la biancheria da letto

to go to bed
andare a letto

to sleep
dormire

to wake up
svegliarsi

to make the bed
fare il letto

to change the sheets
cambiare le lenzuola

GENERAL

blanket
la coperta

bunk beds
i letti a castello

clock radio
la radiosveglia

coat hanger
la gruccia

dressing table
il comò

hairdryer
l'asciugacapelli *m*

laundry basket
il cesto della biancheria

quilt
la trapunta

sheets
le lenzuola

BEDROOM

chest of drawers
la cassettiera

curtains
le tende

mirror
lo specchio

bed
il letto

wardrobe
l'armadio *m*

duvet
il piumone

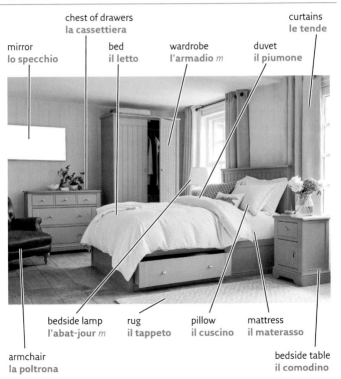

bedside lamp
l'abat-jour *m*

rug
il tappeto

pillow
il cuscino

mattress
il materasso

armchair
la poltrona

bedside table
il comodino

Many Italian homes have more than one bathroom, often a more basic one also used for doing laundry, and a more luxurious main bathroom. It is also quite common to see washing machines installed in the bathroom, rather than in the kitchen or utility room.

VOCABULARY

shower curtain **la tenda da doccia**	drain **lo scarico**	to wash one's hands **lavarsi le mani**
toilet seat **il sedile del gabinetto**	to shower **fare la doccia**	to brush one's teeth **lavarsi i denti**
toiletries **gli articoli per l'igiene personale**	to have a bath **farsi un bagno**	to go to the toilet **andare al gabinetto**

GENERAL

bath mat
il tappetino da bagno

bath towel
l'asciugamano da bagno *m*

face cloth
l'asciugamano per il viso *m*

hand towel
l'asciugamano per le mani *m*

shower puff
la spugna per la doccia

soap
il sapone

sponge
la spugna

toilet brush
lo scopino del water

toilet roll
il rotolo di carta
igienica

BATHROOM

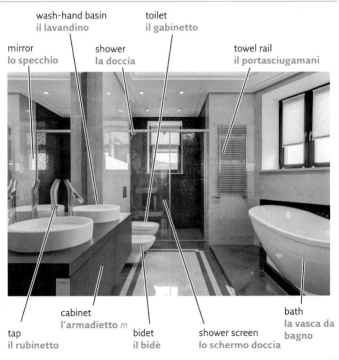

wash-hand basin
il lavandino

toilet
il gabinetto

mirror
lo specchio

shower
la doccia

towel rail
il portasciugamani

tap
il rubinetto

cabinet
l'armadietto *m*

bidet
il bidè

shower screen
lo schermo doccia

bath
la vasca da
bagno

VOCABULARY

tree **l'albero** *m*	flowerbed **l'aiuola** *f*	to weed **rimuovere le erbacce**
soil **il terreno**	compost **il concime**	to water **annaffiare**
grass **l'erba** *f*	allotment **il lotto di terreno**	to grow **coltivare**
plant **la pianta**	gardener **il giardiniere**	to plant **piantare**
weed **l'erbaccia** *f*		

GENERAL

decking
il pavimento in legno

garden fork
il rastrello

garden hose
il tubo da giardino

gardening gloves
i guanti da giardinaggio

garden shed
il capanno da giardino

greenhouse
la serra

hoe
la zappa

lawnmower
il tagliaerba

parasol
il parasole

plant pot
il vaso

pruners
le cesoie da giardiniere

spade
la vanga

trowel
la paletta da giardiniere

watering can
l'annaffiatoio *m*

weedkiller
il diserbante

Wellington boots
gli stivali di gomma

wheelbarrow
la carriola

windowbox
la fioriera

lawn
il prato

shrub
il cespuglio

gate
il cancello

fence
lo steccato

trellis
il traliccio

birdbox
la casetta per
gli uccelli

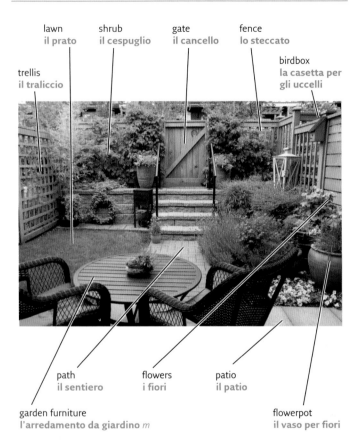

path
il sentiero

flowers
i fiori

patio
il patio

garden furniture
l'arredamento da giardino *m*

flowerpot
il vaso per fiori

VOCABULARY

utility room
il ripostiglio

household appliances
gli elettrodomestici

chores
le faccende

wastepaper basket
il cestino della
spazzatura

basin
la bacinella

bleach
la candeggina

disinfectant
il disinfettante

dishwasher tablet
la pastiglia per la
lavastoviglie

laundry detergent
il detersivo per il
bucato

washing-up liquid
il detersivo per i
piatti

to sweep the floor
spazzare il pavimento

to do the laundry
fare il bucato

to hoover
passare
l'aspirapolvere

to tidy up
mettere a posto

to clean
pulire

to take out the bin
portare fuori la
spazzatura

brush
la scopa

bucket
il secchio

cloth
lo straccio

clothes horse
lo stendino

clothes pegs
le mollette da
bucato

dishwasher
la lavastoviglie

67

dustbin
il bidone della spazzatura

dustpan
la paletta per la spazzatura

iron
il ferro da stiro

ironing board
la tavola da stiro

mop
il mocio

rubber gloves
i guanti di gomma

scourer
la spugna

tea towel
lo strofinaccio

tumble drier
l'asciugatrice *f*

vacuum cleaner
l'aspirapolvere *f*

washing line
il filo del bucato

washing machine
la lavatrice

AT THE SHOPS | NEI NEGOZI

Markets full of lush produce and local specialities, the aroma of freshly baked bread from the panificio, the smell of regional or seasonal specialities coming from a food stall – just some of the things that might spring to mind when it comes to shopping in Italy. That's not to say that you won't find plenty of large supermarkets, busy shopping centres, and many familiar international chains in urban areas.

basket
il cestino

banana
la banana

bread
il pane

vegetable oil
l'olio vegetale *m*

Most stores in Italy are open from Monday to Saturday, and are closed on Sundays, although this is more relaxed than it used to be. Many shops will also shut between 1 p.m. and 3.30 p.m. and stay open in the evening until 7 p.m. or even later.

YOU MIGHT SAY...

Where is the...?
Dov'è il...?

Where is the nearest...?
Dov'è il... più vicino?

Where can I buy...?
Dove posso comprare...?

What time do you open/close?
A che ora aprite / chiudete?

I'm just looking, thanks.
Sto solo dando un'occhiata, grazie.

Do you sell...?
Vendete... ?

May I have...?
Potrei avere...?

Can I pay by cash/card?
Posso pagare in contanti / con la carta?

Can I pay with my mobile app?
Posso pagare con l'app sul cellulare?

How much does this cost?
Quanto costa?

How much is delivery?
Quanto costa la consegna?

I need...
Ho bisogno...

I would like...
Vorrei...

Can I exchange this?
Posso cambiarlo?

Can I get a refund?
Posso avere un rimborso?

That's all, thank you.
Questo è tutto, grazie.

YOU SHOULD KNOW...

Distribution of single-use plastic bags is banned in Italian shops, and since 2018, biodegradable bags have been used for purchases of fresh produce.

Are you being served? **La stanno servendo?**	Can you enter your PIN? **Può digitare il pin?**
Would you like anything else? **Vorrebbe qualcos'altro?**	Would you like a receipt? **Vuole una ricevuta?**
It costs... **Costa...**	We don't offer refunds/exchanges. **Non offriamo rimborsi / cambi.**
I'm sorry, we don't have... **Mi dispiace, non abbiamo...**	Have you got a receipt? **Ha una ricevuta?**
I can order that for you. **Posso ordinarlo.**	Have a good day! **Buona giornata!**
How would you like to pay? **Come vuole pagare?**	

VOCABULARY

shop **il negozio**	change **il resto**	to browse **curiosare**
shopping centre **il centro commerciale**	gift voucher **il buono acquisto**	to buy **acquistare**
supermarket **il supermercato**	PIN **il pin**	to pay **pagare**
market **il mercato**	exchange **il cambio**	to shop (online) **fare compere (online)**
shop assistant **il commesso / la commessa**	refund **il rimborso**	to do the shopping/ go shopping **andare a fare shopping**
cash **i contanti**	voucher **il buono**	
	contactless **contactless**	

banknotes
le banconote

card reader
il lettore carte di credito

coins
le monete

debit/credit card
la carta di debito / credito

paper bag
la busta di carta

plastic bag
la busta di plastica

receipt
la ricevuta

reusable shopping bag
la busta riciclabile

till point
la cassa

Shopping for groceries over the internet is much less prevalent in Italy than in the UK, but some stores in some areas are starting to introduce the service. There are not many 24-hour shops and supermarkets in Italy, although they are becoming more common in the bigger cities.

YOU MIGHT SAY...

Where can I find...?
Dove posso trovare... ?

I'm looking for...
Sto cercando...

Do you have...?
Avete... ?

YOU MIGHT HEAR...

It's in aisle 1/2/3.
È nel corridoio numero 1 / 2 / 3.

Can I help you with your bags?
Posso aiutarla con le buste?

There is a charge for a carrier bag.
La busta ha un costo.

VOCABULARY

groceries **le cibarie**	carton **la confezione**	fresh **fresco**
aisle **il corridoio**	jar **il vasetto**	frozen **congelato**
delicatessen **il negozio di gastronomia**	multipack **confezione multipla** *f*	dairy **ricavato dal latte**
ready meal **il cibo pronto**	packet **il pacchetto**	low-fat **a basso contenuto di grassi**
bottle **la bottiglia**	tin **il barattolo**	low-calorie **a basso contenuto calorico**
box **la scatola**	tinned **in scatola**	

YOU SHOULD KNOW...

Italy has introduced a trial deposit return scheme for glass bottles bought in shops and in restaurants, bars, and hotels.

GENERAL

basket
il cestino

scales
la bilancia

trolley
il carrello

GROCERIES

biscuits
i biscotti

couscous
il couscous

herbs
le erbe aromatiche

honey
il miele

icing sugar
lo zucchero a velo

instant coffee
il caffè solubile

jam
la marmellata

ketchup
il ketchup

marmalade
la marmellata di agrumi

mayonnaise
la maionese

noodles
i noodles

olive oil
l'olio di oliva *m*

pasta
la pasta

pepper
il pepe

rice
il riso

salt
il sale

spices
le spezie

sugar
lo zucchero

teabags
le bustine di tè

vegetable oil
l'olio vegetale *m*

vinegar
l'aceto *m*

SNACKS

chocolate
la cioccolata

crisps
le patatine fritte

nuts
la frutta secca

olives
le olive

popcorn
i popcorn

sweets
le caramelle

DRINKS

beer
la birra

fizzy drink
la bevanda gassata

fruit juice
il succo di frutta

spirits
i superalcolici

still/sparkling water
**l'acqua liscia /
gassata** *f*

wine
il vino

76

Most markets will be set up early in the morning and will wind down around lunchtime, although some bigger markets can stay open all day. There you will find all the fresh produce, regional specialities, and organic produce.

YOU MIGHT SAY...

Where is the market?
Dov'è il mercato?

When is market day?
Quand'è giorno di mercato?

A kilo/100 grams of...
Un chilo / 100 grammi di...

Two/Three ..., please.
Due / Tre ..., per favore.

What do I owe you?
Quanto le devo?

YOU MIGHT HEAR...

The market is in the square.
Il mercato è nella piazza.

The market is on a Tuesday.
Il mercato è martedì.

Can I help you?
Posso aiutarla?

Here you go. Anything else?
Ecco qui. Altro?

Here's your change.
Ecco il resto.

VOCABULARY

marketplace
il mercato

traditional production
la produzione tradizionale

flea market
il mercatino

indoor market
il mercato coperto

farmer's market
il mercato degli agricoltori

stall
la bancarella

trader
il commerciante

produce
i prodotti

local
locale

organic
biologico

seasonal
stagionale

home-made
casereccio

YOU SHOULD KNOW...

Haggling would not be expected at the stalls of a fruit and vegetable market; it's a different story at the flea market!

YOU MIGHT SAY...

Do you have...?
Avete... ?

Are they ripe/fresh?
Sono maturi / freschi?

YOU MIGHT HEAR...

What would you like?
Cosa vorrebbe?

Here you go. Anything else?
Ecco qui. Altro?

VOCABULARY

grocer	segment	ripe
il fruttivendolo	**lo spicchio**	**maturo**
juice	skin	unripe
il succo	**la buccia**	**acerbo**
leaf	stone	to chop
la foglia	**il nocciolo**	**sminuzzare**
peel	raw	to dice
la buccia	**crudo**	**tagliare a dadini**
pip	fresh	to grate
il seme	**fresco**	**grattugiare**
rind	rotten	to juice
la scorza	**marcio**	**spremere**
seed	seedless	to peel
il seme	**senza semi**	**sbucciare**

FRUIT

apple
la mela

apricot
l'albicocca *f*

banana
la banana

blackberry
la mora

blueberry
il mirtillo

cherry
la ciliegia

fig
il fico

grape
l'uva *f*

grapefruit
il pompelmo

kiwi fruit
il kiwi

lemon
il limone

mango
il mango

melon
il melone

nectarine
la pescanoce

orange
l'arancia *f*

passion fruit
il frutto della passione

peach
la pesca

pear
la pera

pineapple
l'ananas *m*

plum
la susina

raspberry
il lampone

redcurrant
il ribes rosso

strawberry
la fragola

watermelon
l'anguria *f*

artichoke
il carciofo

asparagus
l'asparago *m*

aubergine
la melanzana

broad beans
le fave

broccoli
il broccolo

cabbage
il cavolo

carrot
la carota

cauliflower
il cavolfiore

celery
il sedano

chilli
il peperoncino

courgette
la zucchina

cucumber
il cetriolo

garlic
l'aglio *m*

green beans
i fagiolini

leek
il porro

mushroom
il fungo

onion
la cipolla

peas
i piselli

potato
la patata

radicchio
il radicchio

red pepper
il peperone rosso

spinach
gli spinaci

squash
la zucca

tomato
il pomodoro

Ask the fishmonger for tips on what is fresh and what is in season.

YOU MIGHT SAY...

How fresh is this fish?
Quanto è fresco il pesce?

I'd like this filleted, please.
Lo vorrei a filetti, per favore.

Can you remove the bones/shells?
Può spinarlo / sgusciarlo?

Is it sustainably caught fish?
È un pesce sostenibile?

YOU MIGHT HEAR...

This fish is fresh/frozen.
Questo pesce è fresco / congelato.

It was landed...
È stato scaricato...

Would you like this filleted?
Vuole che lo faccia a filetti?

VOCABULARY

fishmonger **il pescivendolo**	scales **le squame**	farmed **di allevamento**
(fish)bone **la lisca**	shellfish **il crostaceo**	wild **selvatico**
fillet **il filetto**	shell **il guscio**	salted **salato**
filleted **fatto a filetti**	freshwater **d'acqua dolce**	smoked **affumicato**
roe **le uova di pesce**	saltwater **di mare**	deboned **spinato**

FISH

anchovy
l'acciuga *f*

cod
il merluzzo

herring
l'aringa *f*

lemon sole
la sogliola

mackerel
lo sgombro

salmon
il salmone

sardine
la sardina

salt cod
la baccalà

sea bass
la spigola

sea bream
l'orata *f*

trout
la trota

tuna
il tonno

clam
la vongola

crab
il granchio

crayfish
il gambero d'acqua dolce

lobster
l'aragosta *f*

mussel
la cozza

octopus
il polipo

oyster
l'ostrica *f*

prawn
il gambero

scallop
la capasanta

sea urchin
il riccio

shrimp
il gamberetto

squid
il calamaro

Butchers in Italy are often able to recommend what kind of cuts to buy for the recipes you'd like to try, as well as local specialties they may sell.

YOU MIGHT SAY...

A slice of..., please.
Una fetta di..., per favore.

Can you slice this for me, please?
Può affettare questo, per favore?

Could you prepare this for me, please?
Potrebbe prepararmelo, per favore?

YOU MIGHT HEAR...

Certainly, sir/madam.
Certo, signore / signora.

How much would you like?
Quanto ne vuole?

How many would you like?
Quanti ne vuole?

VOCABULARY

butcher **il macellaio**	lamb **l'agnello** *m*	venison **la carne di cervo**
meat **la carne**	poultry **il pollame**	offal **le frattaglie**
red meat **la carne rossa**	duck **l'anatra** *f*	cooked **cucinato**
white meat **la carne bianca**	goose **l'oca** *f*	raw **crudo**
cold meats **gli affettati**	turkey **il tacchino**	roasted **arrostito**
beef **il manzo**	game **la cacciagione**	organic **biologico**
pork **il maiale**	veal **la carne di vitello**	free-range **ruspante**

beefburger
l'hamburger *m*

chicken breast
il petto di pollo

chop
la costoletta

(cured) sausage
il salame

ham
il prosciutto

hog roast
la porchetta

joint
il tocco di carne

mince
la carne tritata

mortadella
la mortadella

pancetta
la pancetta

sausage
la salsiccia

steak
la bistecca

87

Bread is an essential part of the Italian diet and each region has its own special kinds of bread and rolls. A "panificio" or "panetteria" will sell bread and simple cakes, while for more luxurious cakes you should try a "pasticceria".

YOU MIGHT SAY...

Do you sell...?
Vendete...?

Could I have...?
Posso avere...?

How much are...?
Quanto costano...?

YOU MIGHT HEAR...

Are you being served?
La stanno servendo?

Would you like anything else?
Vuole altro?

I'm sorry, we don't have...
Mi dispiace, non abbiamo...

VOCABULARY

baker **il fornaio**	loaf **la pagnotta**	flour **la farina**
bread **il pane**	slice **la fetta**	gluten-free **senza glutine**
wholemeal bread **il pane integrale**	crust **la crosta**	to bake **cuocere al forno**

YOU SHOULD KNOW...

A range of delicious breakfast pastries is available in many Italian bars, which often also sell sandwiches at lunchtime.

almond biscuits
i biscotti di mandorle

amaretti biscuits
gli amaretti

bread rolls
i panini

cake
la torta

ciabatta
la ciabatta

croissant
il cornetto

custard-filled croissant
il cornetto alla crema

doughnut
la bomba

éclair
il bignè

focaccia
la focaccia

lattice-top pie
la crostata

panettone
il panettone

Cheese is a hugely important part of the Italian diet, with hundreds of regional varieties. You will find many cheeses made from sheep's milk as well as cow's milk, not forgetting traditional mozzarella made from buffalo milk.

VOCABULARY

cheese
il formaggio

blue cheese
il formaggio erborinato

sheep's-milk cheese
il formaggio di pecora

cow's-milk cheese
il formaggio di mucca

cream cheese
il formaggio spalmabile

smoked cheese
il formaggio affumicato

hard cheese
il formaggio a pasta dura

burrata
la burrata

caciocavallo
il caciocavallo

caciotta
la caciotta

Emmenthal
l'emmental *m*

fontina
la fontina

goat's cheese
il formaggio di capra

gorgonzola
il gorgonzola

mascarpone
il mascarpone

mozzarella
la mozzarella

Parmesan
il parmigiano

pecorino
il pecorino

provolone
il provolone

ricotta
la ricotta

scamorza
la scamorza

taleggio
il taleggio

FRESH AND DAIRY PRODUCTS
PRODOTTI FRESCHI E LATTICINI

UHT milk is much more widely used in Italy than in the UK, but it is possible to find fresh milk in the supermarkets. Look for "latte fresco" in the chiller cabinet.

VOCABULARY

egg white
l'albume *m*

egg yolk
il tuorlo

UHT milk
il latte a lunga conservazione

whole milk
il latte intero

semi-skimmed milk
il latte parzialmente scremato

skimmed milk
il latte scremato

double cream
la panna intera

single cream
la panna semigrassa

pasteurized
pastorizzato

unpasteurized
non pastorizzato

free-range
di gallina ruspante

dairy-free
senza lattosio

butter
il burro

cream
la panna

eggs
le uova

margarine
la margarina

milk
il latte

yoghurt
lo yogurt

In Italy, pharmacies are owned and run by individual pharmacists, meaning that you don't see pharmacy chains in Italian towns and villages. Pharmacies operate a rotation system and outside normal opening hours a sign on the door will normally tell you where the nearest open pharmacy is.

YOU MIGHT SAY...

I need something for...
Ho bisogno di qualcosa per...

I'm allergic to...
Sono allergico a...

What would you recommend?
Che cosa mi consiglia?

I'm collecting a prescription.
Devo prendere le medicine in questa ricetta.

Is it suitable for young children?
È adatto per i bambini piccoli?

YOU MIGHT HEAR...

Do you have a prescription?
Ha la ricetta?

Do you have ID?
Ha un documento di identificazione?

Do you have any allergies?
Ha allergie?

Take two tablets twice a day.
Prenda due pasticche due volte al giorno.

You should see a doctor.
Sarebbe meglio se andasse dal dottore.

VOCABULARY

pharmacist **il farmacista**	hay fever **la febbre da fieno**	antihistamine **l'antistaminico** *m*
prescription **la ricetta**	asthma **l'asma** *f*	antiseptic **l'antisettico** *m*
cold **il raffreddore**	headache **il mal di testa**	decongestant **il decongestionante**
diarrhoea **la diarrea**	sore throat/stomach **il mal di gola / stomaco**	painkiller **l'antidolorifico** *m*

antiseptic cream
la crema antisettica

bandage
la fasciatura

capsule
la capsula

condom
il preservativo

cough mixture
lo sciroppo per la tosse

drops
le gocce

insect repellent
l'insettifugo *m*

lozenge
la losanga

medicine
la medicina

plaster
il cerotto

suntan lotion
la crema solare

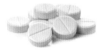
tablet/pill
la pastiglia

antiperspirant
l'antitraspirante *m*

conditioner
il balsamo

mouthwash
il collutorio

razor
il rasoio

sanitary towel
l'assorbente *m*

shampoo
lo shampoo

shaving foam
la schiuma da barba

shower gel
il bagnoschiuma

soap
il sapone

tampon
l'assorbente interno *m*

toothbrush
lo spazzolino da denti

toothpaste
il dentifricio

blusher
il fard

comb
il pettine

eyeliner
l'eye liner *m*

eyeshadow
l'ombretto *m*

foundation
il fondotinta

hairbrush
la spazzola per capelli

hairspray
lo spray per capelli

lip balm
il burro cacao

lipstick
il rossetto

mascara
il mascara

nail varnish
lo smalto per le unghie

powder
la terra

If you intend to travel to Italy with a baby, it may be possible to hire the
equipment you require from specialist companies.

VOCABULARY

sterilizer **lo sterilizzatore**	teething gel **il gel dentizione**	to sterilize **sterilizzare**
disposable nappy **il pannolino usa e getta**	nappy rash **l'eritema da pannolino** *f*	to be teething **mettere i denti**
nappy sacks **i sacchetti per pannolini**	colic **la colica**	to breast-feed **allattare**

CLOTHING

babygro®/sleepsuit
la tutina

bib
il bavaglino

bootees
le scarpine

mittens
le muffole

snowsuit
il pagliaccetto

vest
la canottiera

baby food
gli omogeneizzati

baby lotion
la crema per bambini

baby's bottle
il biberon

changing bag
la borsa per il cambio

cotton bud
il cotton fioc

cotton wool
l'ovatta *f*

formula milk
il latte in polvere

nappy
il pannolino

nappy cream
la crema per eritema da pannolino

rusk
il biscotto

talcum powder
il borotalco

wet wipes
le salviette umidificate

baby bath
la vaschetta per il bagnetto

baby seat
il sedile per bambini

baby walker
il girello

cot
il lettino

dummy
il ciuccio

highchair
il seggiolone

mobile
la giostrina

Moses basket
la culla di vimini

pram
la carrozzina

pushchair
il passeggino

teething ring
l'anello da dentizione *m*

travel cot
il lettino da viaggio

A large T on a sign outside a shop or bar in Italy indicates that it sells tobacco, stamps, and tickets for local public transport.

VOCABULARY

broadsheet
il giornale

tabloid
il giornale scandalistico

kiosk
il chiosco

stationery
la cartoleria

tickets
i biglietti

tobacconist
la tabaccheria

vendor
il venditore

daily
giornaliero

weekly
settimanale

GENERAL

book
il libro

cigar
il sigaro

cigarette
la sigaretta

comic book
il libro di fumetti

confectionery
i dolciumi

envelope
la busta

greetings card
il biglietto d'auguri

magazine
la rivista

map
la mappa

newspaper
il giornale

notebook
il taccuino

pen
la penna

pencil
la matita

postcard
la cartolina

puzzle book
il libro di enigmistica

scratch card
il gratta e vinci

stamp
il francobollo

tobacco
il tabacco

You will find department stores such as La Rinascente and Coin in several Italian cities. For a different shopping experience, try the world's oldest shopping mall, the stunning Galleria Vittorio Emanuele in Milan, or its Neapolitan equivalent, the Galleria Umberto 1.

YOU MIGHT SAY...

Where is the menswear department?
Dov'è il reparto abbigliamento uomo?

Which floor is this?
Che piano è questo?

Can you gift-wrap this, please?
Può fare una confezione regalo, per favore?

YOU MIGHT HEAR...

Menswear is on the second floor.
L'abbigliamento uomo è al secondo piano.

This is the first floor.
Questo è il primo piano.

Would you like this gift-wrapped?
Vuole che le faccio una confezione regalo?

VOCABULARY

floor
il piano

escalator
la scala mobile

lift
l'ascensore *m*

toilets
la toilette

counter
il bancone

department
il reparto

menswear
l'abbigliamento uomo *m*

womenswear
l'abbigliamento donna *m*

sportswear
l'abbigliamento sportivo *m*

swimwear
i costumi da bagno

brand
la marca

designer
di marca

luxury
di lusso

sale
i saldi

accessories
gli accessori

cosmetics
i cosmetici

fashion
la moda

food and drink
cibo e bevande

footwear
le calzature

furniture
i mobili

kitchenware
gli utensili da cucina

leather goods
gli articoli in pelle

lighting
l'illuminazione *f*

lingerie
la biancheria intima

soft furnishings
i tessuti d'arredo

toys
i giocattoli

Italy is famous for fashion and every city has at least one elegant street dedicated to designer shops. More affordable fashions can be found in the many street markets or individually owned boutiques.

YOU MIGHT SAY...

I'm just looking, thanks.
Sto solo dando un'occhiata, grazie.

I'd like to try this on, please.
Vorrei provare questo per favore.

Where are the fitting rooms?
Dove sono i camerini?

I'm a size...
Sono una...

Have you got a bigger/smaller size? (clothing)
Ha una taglia più grande / piccola?

Have you got a bigger/smaller size? (shoes)
Ha un numero più grande / piccolo?

This is too small/big.
È troppo piccolo / grande.

This is too short.
Questo è troppo corto.

This is torn.
È strappato.

YOU MIGHT HEAR...

Can I help you?
Posso aiutarla?

Let me know if I can help.
Mi faccia sapere se posso aiutarla.

The fitting rooms are over there.
I camerini sono là.

What size are you? (clothing)
Che taglia porta?

What size are you? (shoes)
Che numero di scarpe?

I can get you another size.
Le posso prendere un'altra taglia.

I'm sorry, it's out of stock.
Mi dispiace, è terminato.

I'm sorry, we don't have that size/colour.
Mi dispiace, non abbiamo quella taglia / colore.

That suits you.
Le sta bene.

VOCABULARY

fitting room **il camerino**	umbrella **l'ombrello** *m*	leather **la pelle**
clothes/clothing **gli abiti**	casual **casual**	silk **la seta**
shoes/footwear **le calzature**	smart **elegante**	size (clothing) **la taglia**
underwear **l'abbigliamento intimo** *m*	wool **la lana**	size (shoe) **il numero**
wallet **il portafoglio**	denim **il denim**	petite **petite**
purse **il borsellino**	cotton **il cotone**	plus-size **taglie forti**
jewellery **i gioielli**	polyester **il poliestere**	to try on **provare**

CLOTHING

bikini
il bikini

blouse
la camicetta

boxer shorts
i boxer

bra
il reggiseno

cardigan
il cardigan

coat
il cappotto

dress
l'abito *m*

dressing gown
la vestaglia

jacket
la giacca

jeans
i jeans

jogging bottoms
la tuta da ginnastica

jumper
il maglione

leggings
i pantacollant

pants
le mutande

pyjamas
il pigiama

shirt
la camicia

shorts
i calzoncini

skirt
la gonna

socks
i calzini

sweatshirt
la felpa

swimsuit
il costume da bagno

(three-piece) suit
l'abito (a tre pezzi) *m*

tie
la cravatta

tights
il collant

trousers
i pantaloni

T-shirt
la T-shirt

waterproof jacket
la giacca impermeabile

ACCESSORIES

baseball cap
il berretto con visiera

belt
la cinta

bracelet
il bracciale

earrings
gli orecchini *mpl*

gloves
i guanti

handbag
la borsa

necklace
la collana

scarf
la sciarpa

woolly hat
il cappello di lana

FOOTWEAR

boots
gli stivali

high heels
i tacchi alti

lace-up shoes
le scarpe stringate

sandals
i sandali

slippers
le pantofole

trainers
le scarpe da ginnastica

From local retail and trade merchants to numerous larger chain stores, there are many options available for those who are looking for some DIY essentials.

VOCABULARY

tool **l'utensile** *m*	electricity **l'elettricità** *f*	painting **l'imbiancatura** *f*
tool box **la cassetta degli attrezzi**	joinery **la carpenteria**	plumbing **la piombatura**
power tool **l'utensile elettrico** *m*	home improvements **il fai da te**	to do DIY **faire il fai da te**

chisel
lo scalpello

electric drill
il trapano elettrico

hammer
il martello

nails
i chiodi

nuts and bolts
i dadi e bulloni

paint
la vernice

paintbrush
il pennello

paint roller
il rullo per verniciare

pliers
le pinze

saw
la sega

screwdriver
il cacciavite

screws
le viti

spanner
il chiave inglese

spirit level
la livella

stepladder
la scala a libretto

tiles
le mattonelle

wallpaper
la carta da parati

wrench
la chiave

antique shop
l'antiquariato *m*

barber's
il barbiere

beauty salon
il salone di bellezza

bookshop
la libreria

boutique
la boutique

car showroom
l'autosalone *m*

deli
la pizzicheria

electronics store
il negozio di elettronica

estate agency
l'agenzia immobiliare *f*

florist's
il fioraio

furniture store
il negozio di mobili

garden centre
il vivaio

hairdresser's
il parrucchiere

health food shop
il negozio di alimenti naturali

jeweller's shop
l'orefice *m*

optician's
l'ottico *m*

pet shop
il negozio di animali

phone shop
il negozio di telefoni

record shop
il negozio di musica

shoe shop
il negozio di scarpe

shopping mall
il centro commerciale

toyshop
il negozio di giocattoli

travel agency
l'agenzia viaggi *f*

wine shop
l'enoteca *f*

Business meetings, meals with friends, or courses of study... whatever your day-to-day schedule looks like during your time in Italy, this section deals with the words and phrases you may require when going on errands, planning outings, and going about your everyday business.

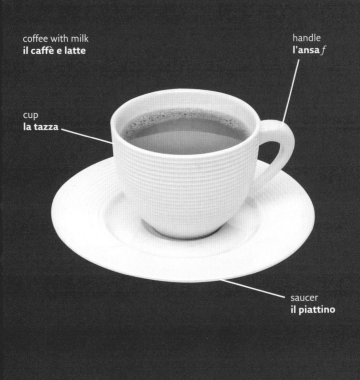

coffee with milk
il caffè e latte

handle
l'ansa *f*

cup
la tazza

saucer
il piattino

Here are a few basic words and phrases for describing your day-to-day routine ("la vita quotidiana") and making plans with others.

YOU MIGHT SAY...

Where are you going?
Dove stai andando?

What time do you finish?
A che ora finisci?

What are you doing today/tonight?
Che fai oggi / stasera?

Are you free on Friday?
Sei libero venerdì?

Would you like to meet up?
Ti va di vederci?

Where/When would you like to meet?
Dove / Quando ti va di vederci?

YOU MIGHT HEAR...

I'm at work/uni.
Sono al lavoro / all'università.

I have a day off.
Ho il giorno libero.

I've got an appointment.
Ho un appuntamento.

I'm going to...
Sto andando a...

I'll be back by...
Torno alle...

I'll meet you at...
Ci vediamo a/in...

I can't meet up then, sorry.
Allora non ci possiamo vedere, scusa.

VOCABULARY

to wake up **svegliarsi**	to arrive **arrivare**	to meet friends **incontrare gli amici**
to get dressed **vestirsi**	to leave **partire**	to go home **andare a casa**
to eat **mangiare**	to study **studiare**	to go to bed **andare a letto**
to drink **bere**	to work **lavorare**	

In Italy, breakfast tends to be a smaller, lighter meal than it is in other countries. Most Italian people will eat breakfast at home, although some like to have breakfast in a bar.

VOCABULARY

bread and butter **pane con burro**	to have breakfast **fare colazione**	to skip breakfast **saltare la colazione**

YOU SHOULD KNOW...

The crescent-shaped "cornetto" is a popular choice for breakfast when in a bar, either plain or filled ("ripieno") with jam or confectioner's custard ("crema"). Cappuccino is only drunk in the morning, and never after a meal, when an espresso is preferred.

DRINKS

cappuccino
il cappuccino

coffee
il caffè

espresso
l'espresso *m*

hot chocolate
la cioccolata calda

orange juice
il succo d'arancia

tea
il tè

bread rolls
i panini

butter
il burro

cereal
i cereali

chocolate spread
la cioccolata da spalmare

crispbread
la fetta biscottata

croissant
il cornetto

fruit salad
la macedonia

jam
la marmellata

muesli
il muesli

Lunch is often seen as the most important meal of the day in Italy and it usually involves two courses plus fruit. Many shops and businesses close for at least two hours for lunch and people will often go home to eat if they live nearby.

YOU MIGHT SAY...

What's for dinner?
Che c'è per cena?

What time is lunch?
A che ora è il pranzo?

May I have...?
Posso avere...?

Can I try it?
Posso provarlo?

YOU MIGHT HEAR...

We're having ... for dinner.
Per cena c'è...

Lunch is at midday.
Il pranzo è a mezzogiorno.

Dinner's ready!
La cena è pronta!

Would you like...?
Vuole...?

VOCABULARY

lunch **il pranzo**	recipe **la ricetta**	to have lunch **pranzare**
dinner **la cena**	aperitif **l'aperitivo** *m*	to have dinner **cenare**
courses **le portate**	after-dinner drink **il digestivo**	to eat out **mangiare fuori**

YOU SHOULD KNOW...

Italians don't tend to graze between meals, but children will often have an afternoon snack, known as "una merenda".

APPETIZERS

assorted cold meats
and cheeses
**gli affettati e
formaggi misti**

cream soup
la vellutata

deep-fried rice balls
gli arancini

fried courgette flowers
**i fiori di zucca in
pastella**

mixed seafood
**il piatto misto di
mare**

smoked salmon
**il salmone
affumicato**

FIRST COURSES

fish soup
la zuppa di pesce

lasagne
le lasagne

pasta
la pasta

risotto
il risotto

soup
la zuppa

tortellini
i tortellini

grilled sea bream
l'orata alla griglia *f*

meatballs in tomato
sauce
le polpette al sugo

meat roulade
il rollè *m*

pork cutlet
**la costoletta di
maiale**

roast chicken
il pollo al forno

sliced beef
la fettina di manzo

sliced veal in tuna sauce
il vitello tonnato

sirloin steak
la bistecca

veal wrapped in Parma
ham and sage
il saltinbocca

SIDES

chips
le patatine fritte

green salad
l'insalata verde *f*

mixed salad
l'insalata mista *f*

roast potatoes
le patate arrosto

spinach with lemon
and olive oil
gli spinaci all'agro

stir-fried chicory
**la cicoria ripassata
in padella**

DESSERTS

apple cake
la torta di mele

chocolate mousse
**la mousse al
cioccolato**

custard tart with pine
nuts
la torta della nonna

fruit tart
**la crostatina alla
frutta**

ice cream
il gelato

pannacotta
la panna cotta

parfait
il semifreddo

profiteroles
i profiteroles

tiramisu
il tiramisù

Italy is renowned the world over for its cuisine, so it goes without saying that eating out is an important social experience in Italian culture.

YOU MIGHT SAY...

I'd like to make a reservation.
Vorrei prenotare.

A table for four, please.
Un tavolo per quattro, per favore.

We're ready to order.
Siamo pronti a ordinare.

What would you recommend?
Che cosa consiglia?

What are the specials today?
Quali sono i piatti del giorno?

May I have ..., please?
Posso avere ..., per favore?

Are there vegetarian/vegan options?
Ci sono piatti vegetariani / vegetaliani?

I'm allergic to...
Sono allergico a...

Excuse me, this is cold.
Mi scusi, questo è freddo.

This is not what I ordered.
Questo non è quello che ho ordinato.

May we have the bill, please?
Ci porta il conto, per favore?

YOU MIGHT HEAR...

At what time?
A che ora?

How many people?
Quante persone?

Sorry, we're fully booked.
Mi dispiace, siamo pieni.

Would you like anything to drink?
Vuoi qualcosa da bere?

Are you ready to order?
Siete pronti a ordinare?

I'd recommend...
Consiglierei...

The specials today are...
I piatti del giorno sono...

I will let the chef know.
Lo farò sapere allo chef.

Enjoy your meal!
Buon appetito!

VOCABULARY

set menu **il menù fisso**	vegetarian **vegetariano**	to reserve a table **prenotare un tavolo**
daily specials **le specialità del giorno**	vegan **vegetaliano**	to order **ordinare**
service charge **il coperto**	gluten-free **senza glutine**	to ask for the bill **chiedere il conto**
tip **la mancia**	dairy-free **senza lattosio**	to be served **essere servito**

YOU SHOULD KNOW...

Bread is usually provided in Italian restaurants as part of a small cover charge ("pane e coperto"). It's considered polite to tear the bread with your hands rather than cutting it, and aside from in the most formal restaurants, it's acceptable to use it to mop up the sauce from your meal ("fare la scarpetta").

GENERAL

bar
il bancone

bill
il conto

bread basket
il cestino del pane

chair
la sedia

cheese knife
il coltello da formaggio

fish knife
il coltello da pesce

menu
il menù

jug of water
la caraffa d'acqua

salt and pepper
il sale e il pepe

steak knife
il coltello da carne

table
il tavolo

tablecloth
la tovaglia

toothpicks
gli stuzzicadenti

vinegar and oil
l'aceto e l'olio *m*

waiter/waitress
**il cameriere /
la cameriera**

side plate
il piattino

butter knife
il coltello da burro

dessert spoon
il cucchiaio da dolce

white wine glass
il bicchiere da vino bianco

dessert fork
la forchetta da dolce

water glass
il bicchiere per l'acqua

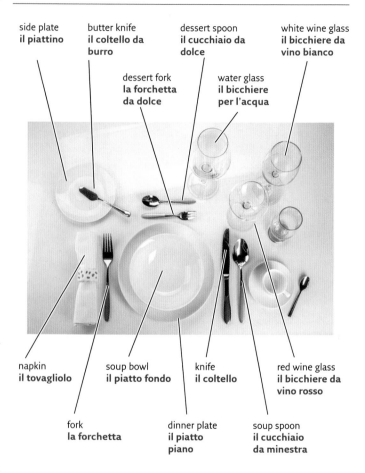

napkin
il tovagliolo

soup bowl
il piatto fondo

knife
il coltello

red wine glass
il bicchiere da vino rosso

fork
la forchetta

dinner plate
il piatto piano

soup spoon
il cucchiaio da minestra

Pizza, the original fast food, was invented in Naples, but there are plenty of other options for eating on the go.

YOU MIGHT SAY...

I'd like to order, please.
Vorrei ordinare, per favore.

Do you deliver?
Fate servizio a domicilio?

I'm sitting in/taking away.
Mangio qui. / Porto via.

How long will it be?
Quanto tempo ci vorrà?

Is there a charge for delivery
C'è qualcosa da pagare per la spedizione?

That's everything, thanks.
Questo è tutto, grazie.

YOU MIGHT HEAR...

Can I help you?
Posso aiutarla?

Sit-in or takeaway?
Mangia qui o porta via?

Small, medium or large?
Piccolo, medio o grande?

We do/don't do delivery.
Facciamo / Non facciamo servizio a domicilio.

Would you like anything else?
Vuole altro?

VOCABULARY

fast-food chain
la catena di fast food

food stall
il banco

vendor
il venditore / la venditrice

drive-thru
il drive-in

an order to go/ a takeaway
un ordine a portar via

delivery charge
le spese di spedizione

delivery man/woman
l'addetto alle consegne *m* /
l'addetta alle consegne *f*

to place an order
ordinare

to collect an order
prendere un'ordinazione

to phone in an order
ordinare per telefono

fries
le patatine fritte

burger
l'hamburger *m*

hot dog
l'hot dog *m*

omelette
l'omelette *f*

pancakes
le crêpes

panini
il panino

pizza
la pizza

sushi
il sushi

toasted sandwich
il toast

Technology plays a huge role in people's everyday lives. A mere click, tap, or swipe helps us to stay in touch with friends and family, keep up to date with what's going on, and find the information we need.

YOU MIGHT SAY/HEAR...

I'll give you a call later.
Richiamo più tardi.

I'll email you.
Le mando un'email.

Can you text me?
Può mandarmi un messaggio?

Can I call you back?
Posso richiamarla?

This is a bad line.
Questa linea è disturbata.

I don't have any signal.
Non ho segnale.

May I have your email address?
Posso avere il suo indirizzo email?

What's your number?
Qual'è il suo numero di telefono?

The website address is...
L'indirizzo del il sito web è...

What's the WiFi password?
Qual'è la password per il wi-fi?

It's all one word.
È tutta una parola.

It's upper/lower case.
Si scrive con la maiuscola / con la minuscola.

VOCABULARY

post **il messaggio**	internet **il internet**	icon **l'icona** *f*
social media **i social media**	WiFi **il wi-fi**	mouse **il mouse**
email **l'email** *f*	website **il sito web**	mouse mat **il tappetino mouse**
email address **l'indirizzo email** *m*	link **il link**	keyboard **la tastiera**

app
l'applicazione f

data
i dati

mobile phone
il (telefono) cellulare

landline
il telefono fisso

phone call
la telefonata

text message
il messaggio SMS

phone signal
il segnale telefonico

voice mail
la segreteria telefonica

touchscreen
lo schermo tattile

screen
il monitor

button
il tasto

battery
la batteria

cable
il cavo

to make a phone call
fare una telefonata

to leave a voice mail
lasciare un messaggio in segreteria

to post (online)
postare

to download/upload
scaricare / caricare

to charge your phone
ricaricare il telefono

to switch on/off
accendere / spegnere

to click on
cliccare su

charger
il caricabatterie

computer
il computer

SIM card
la SIM

smartphone
lo smartphone

tablet
il tablet

wireless router
il router senza fili

Compulsory education in Italy begins at age six and continues to age 16. Nursery schooling is optional, but most parents choose to send their children to nursery school between the ages of three and six.

YOU MIGHT SAY...

What are you studying?
Che cosa studi?

What year are you in?
Che classe fai?

What's your favourite subject?
Qual'è la tua materia preferita?

YOU MIGHT HEAR...

I'm studying...
Studio...

I'm in Year 6/my final year.
Faccio la quinta elementare / l'ultimo anno.

I have an assignment.
Devo fare i compiti.

VOCABULARY

nursery school
la scuola materna

primary school
la scuola elementare

secondary school
la scuola secondaria di primo e di secondo grado

college
l'università *f*

university
l'università *f*

headteacher
il preside

teacher
il professore / la professoressa

janitor
il bidello / la bidella

pupil
l'alunno *m* / **l'alunna** *f*

classroom
la classe

timetable
l'orario *m*

lesson
la lezione

lecture
la lezione

tutorial
la lezione

assignment
l'assegnazione *f*

homework
i compiti

exam
l'esame *m*

degree
la laurea

undergraduate
l'universitario *m* / **l'universitaria** *f*

postgraduate
il postlaureato / la postlaureata

canteen **la mensa**	student union **l'associazione studentesca** *f*	to revise **rivedere**
assembly hall **l'aula magna** *f*	to learn **imparare**	to sit an exam **sostenere un esame**
playing field **il campo da gioco**	to read **leggere**	to graduate **laurearsi**
halls of residence **gli alloggi per studenti universitari**	to write **scrivere**	to study **studiare**
matriculation card **la carta di immatricolazione**	to teach **insegnare**	

SCHOOL

colouring pencils
le matite colorate

eraser
la gomma da cancellare

exercise book
il quaderno

paper
la carta

pen
la penna

pencil
la matita

pencil case
l'astuccio *m*

ruler
il righello

schoolbag
lo zaino

sharpener
il temperamatite

textbook
il libro di testo

whiteboard
la lavagna bianca

HIGHER EDUCATION

cafeteria
la caffetteria

campus
il campus

lecture hall
l'aula *f*

lecturer
il docente

library
la biblioteca

student
**lo studente /
la studentessa**

131

Office hours tend to be from 8–9 a.m. to 6–7 p.m. Many businesses will have a lunch break of between 90 minutes and two hours.

YOU MIGHT SAY/HEAR...

Can we arrange a meeting?
Possiamo organizzare un meeting?

He/She can't come to the phone.
Non può venire al telefono.

May I ask who's calling?
Potrei sapere chi parla?

May I speak to...?
Posso parlare con...?

I have a meeting with...
Ho un meeting con...

I'll email the files to you.
Le mando i file via email.

Mr/Ms ... is on the phone.
Il signor / La signora ... è al telefono.

Here's my business card.
Questo è il mio biglietto da visita.

YOU SHOULD KNOW...

At lunchtime, eating at one's office desk rather than taking a break with colleagues can be seen as unusual.

VOCABULARY

manager
**il direttore /
la direttrice**

staff
il personale

colleague
il collega / la collega

client
il cliente

human resources
le risorse umane

accounts
la contabilità

figures
le cifre

spreadsheet
il foglio elettronico

presentation
la presentazione

report
la relazione

meeting
la riunione

conference call
la teleconferenza

video conference
la videoconferenza

ink cartridge
**la cartuccia
d'inchiostro**

inbox
la posta in arrivo

file
il file

password
la password

to give a presentation
fare una presentazione

attachment
l'allegato *m*

to log on/off
connettersi / disconnettersi

to hold a meeting
organizzare una riunione

username
il nome utente

to type
battere (a macchina)

calculator
la calcolatrice

desk
la scrivania

desk lamp
la lampada da tavolo

filing cabinet
lo schedario

folder
la cartella

hole punch
la perforatrice

in/out tray
la vaschetta portacorrispondenza

laptop
il portatile

notepad
il taccuino

paper clip
la graffetta

photocopier
la fotocopiatrice

printer
la stampante

ring binder
il raccoglitore ad anelli

scanner
lo scanner

scissors
le forbici

stapler
la spillatrice

sticky notes
i Post-it®

sticky tape
lo scotch®

swivel chair
la sedia girevole

telephone
il telefono

USB stick
la chiavetta USB

Most banks are open during normal business hours from Monday to Friday, and on Saturday mornings, though this will vary.

YOU MIGHT SAY...

I'd like to...
Vorrei...

... open an account.
... aprire un conto.

... apply for a loan/mortgage.
... chiedere un prestito / mutuo.

... register for online banking.
... registrarmi per il servizio bancario telematico.

Is there a fee for this service?
Questo servizio ha un costo?

I need to cancel my debit/credit card.
Devo annullare la mia carta di debito / credito.

YOU MIGHT HEAR...

May I see your ID, please?
Potrei vedere un suo documento d'identità, per favore?

How much would you like to withdraw/deposit?
Quanto vuole depositare / prelevare?

Could you enter your PIN, please?
Può digitare il pin, per favore?

You must fill out an application form.
Deve riempire un modulo.

You must make an appointment.
Deve prendere un appuntamento.

There is a fee for this service.
Questo servizio ha un costo.

VOCABULARY

branch **la filiale**	bank account **il conto bancario**	account number **il numero di conto**
cashier **il cassiere / la cassiera**	current account **il conto corrente**	bank statement **l'estratto conto** *m*
online banking **i servizi bancari online**	savings account **il libretto di risparmio**	bank balance **il saldo bancario**

overdraft	currency	to borrow
lo scoperto	**la moneta**	**prendere in prestito**
bank transfer	loan	to repay
il bonifico bancario	**il prestito**	**ripagare**
chequebook	mortgage	to withdraw
il blocchetto degli assegni	**il mutuo**	**prelevare**
	interest	to change money
	l'interesse *m*	**cambiare dei soldi**

If using a foreign debit card whilst in Italy, most cash machines will give you the option of carrying out transactions in another language.

ATM
lo sportello bancomat

banknotes
le banconote

bureau de change
l'ufficio di cambio *m*

debit/credit card
la carta di debito / credito

exchange rate
il tasso di cambio

safety deposit box
la cassetta di sicurezza

Opening hours for post offices are 8.30 a.m. to 7 p.m. on weekdays, and 8.30 a.m. to 1 p.m. on Saturdays. Be aware that some postboxes will have one slot for local mail ("per la città") and one for destinations further afield.

YOU MIGHT SAY...

I'd like to send this first-class/ by airmail.
Vorrei spedirlo con la posta prioritaria / per posta aerea.

Can I get a certificate of postage, please?
Posso avere un certificato di spedizione, per favore?

How long will delivery take?
Quando è prevista la consegna?

I'd like a book of stamps, please.
Vorrei una confezione di francobolli, per favore.

YOU MIGHT HEAR...

Place it on the scales, please.
Lo metta sulla bilancia, per favore.

What are the contents?
Cosa contiene?

What is the value of this parcel?
Qual'è il valore di questo pacco?

Would you like a certificate of postage?
Vuole un certificato di spedizione?

How many stamps do you require?
Di quanti francobolli ha bisogno?

VOCABULARY

address **l'indirizzo** *m*	postal van **il furgone della posta**	airmail **la posta aerea**
first-class **la posta prioritaria**	courier **il corriere**	to post **imbucare**
second-class **la posta ordinaria**	mail **la posta**	to send **inviare**

YOU SHOULD KNOW...

The Vatican has its own postal system, with its own stamps.

box
la scatola

envelope
la busta

letter
la lettera

package
il pacco

padded envelope
la busta imbottita

postal worker
l'impiegato postale *m* /
l'impiegata postale *f*

postbox
la buca delle lettere

postcard
la cartolina

stamp
il francobollo

YOU MIGHT SAY...

How do I get to the city centre?
Come arrivo in centro?

I need to go to...
Devo andare a...

I'd like to visit...
Vorrei visitare...

What are the opening hours?
Quali sono gli orari di apertura?

YOU MIGHT HEAR...

It's open between ... and...
È aperto tra ... e...

It's closed on Mondays.
Il lunedì è chiuso.

PLACES OF IMPORTANCE

café
il bar

cathedral
la cattedrale

church
la chiesa

conference centre
il centro conferenze

courthouse
il tribunale

fire station
**la caserma dei vigili
del fuoco**

fountain
la fontana

hospital
l'ospedale *m*

hotel
l'albergo *m*

laundrette
la lavanderia

library
la biblioteca

mosque
la moschea

office block
gli uffici

park
il parco

playground
il parco giochi

police station
il commissariato

synagogue
la sinagoga

town hall
il municipio

A day trip, a break away, a night out, maybe even a night in – we all like to spend our time differently. It's also a common topic of conversation with friends and colleagues; who doesn't like talking about holidays, hobbies, and how they like to hang out?

tent
la tenda

guy rope
la corda da campeggio

flysheet
il telone esterno

groundsheet
il telone impermeabile

tent peg
il picchetto da tenda

YOU MIGHT SAY...

What would you like to do?
Cosa vorresti fare?

What do you do in your spare time?
Che fai nel tempo libero?

Have you got any hobbies?
Hai degli hobby?

Do you enjoy...?
Ti piace...?

Are you sporty/creative?
Sei sportivo / creativo?

Are you going on holiday this year?
Vai in vacanza quest'anno?

How did you get into...?
Come ti sei interessato a...?

YOU MIGHT HEAR...

My hobbies include...
Alcuni dei miei hobby sono...

I like...
Mi piace...

I really enjoy it.
Mi diverte molto.

It's not for me.
Non è per me.

I'm going on holiday.
Vado in vacanza.

I am sporty/creative.
Sono sportivo / creativo.

I have/don't have a lot of spare time.
Ho / Non ho molto tempo libero.

VOCABULARY

spare time il tempo libero	keen entusiasta	to relax rilassarsi
activity le attività	fun divertente	to enjoy oneself divertirsi
hobby l'hobby *m*	boring noioso	to get bored annoiarsi
pastime il passatempo	to be interested in essere interessato a	
holiday la vacanza	to pass the time passare il tempo	

cooking
la cucina

DIY
il fai da te

gaming
giocare ai
videogiochi

gardening
il giardinaggio

jogging
il jogging

listening to music
ascoltare la musica

reading
la lettura

shopping
fare shopping

sports
lo sport

travelling
il viaggio

walking
il camminare

watching TV/films
guardare la TV /
i film

Italy is one of the most popular tourist destinations in the world – given the wealth of sightseeing opportunities it offers, it's easy to see why.

YOU MIGHT SAY...

How much is it to get in?
Quant'è l'entrata?

Is there a discount for students/ seniors?
C'è uno sconto per studenti / persone anziane?

Where is the tourist office?
Dov'è l'ufficio turistico?

Are there sightseeing tours?
Ci sono visite guidate?

Are there audio guides available?
Avete audio-guide disponibili?

YOU MIGHT HEAR...

Entry costs...
L'entrata costa...

There is/isn't a discount available.
C'è / Non c'è uno sconto.

The tourist office is located...
L'ufficio turistico si trova...

You can book a guided tour.
Può prenotare una visita guidata.

Audio guides are/are not available.
Ci sono / Non ci sono audio guide disponibili.

VOCABULARY

tourist il turista	nature reserve la riserva naturale	guided tour la visita guidata
tourist attraction l'attrazione turistica *f*	historic site il sito storico	to visit visitare
excursion l'escursione *f*	audio guide l'audio-guida *f*	to see vedere

YOU SHOULD KNOW...

Bear in mind that many cultural and historical sites, including most museums and art galleries, are closed on Mondays. Many restaurants close on Mondays too, so check before you visit.

art gallery
la galleria d'arte

camera
la macchinetta fotografica

castle
il castello

cathedral
la cattedrale

city map
la mappa della città

gardens
i giardini

guidebook
la guida

monument
il monumento

museum
il museo

sightseeing bus
l'autobus turistico *m*

tour guide
la guida turistica

tourist office
l'ufficio turistico *m*

When it comes to nightlife in Italy's towns and cities, check the local tourist office for information on local events and venues. Why not get recommendations on bars and clubs from residents, too?

YOU MIGHT SAY...

What is there to do at night?
Cosa c'è da fare la sera?

What's on at the cinema/theatre?
Che c'è al cinema / teatro?

Where are the best bars/clubs?
Dove sono i migliori locali / club?

Do you want to go for a drink?
Vuoi andare a bere qualcosa?

Do you want to go and see a film/show?
Vuoi andare al cinema / teatro?

Are there tickets for...?
Ci sono dei biglietti per...?

Two seats in the stalls/balcony, please.
Due posti in platea / in balconata, per favore.

What time does it start?
A che ora inizia?

I enjoyed myself.
Mi sono divertito.

YOU MIGHT HEAR...

The nightlife is/isn't great around here.
La vita notturna è / non è un granché qui.

My favourite bar/club is...
Il mio locale / club preferito è...

I'm going for a few drinks/to the theatre.
Vado a bere qualcosa / a teatro.

There's a film/show I'd like to see.
C'è un film / uno spettacolo che mi piacerebbe vedere.

There are tickets left.
Ci sono ancora dei biglietti.

There are no tickets left.
Non ci sono più biglietti.

It begins at 7 o'clock.
Inizia alle 7.

Please turn off your mobile phones.
Per favore, spegnete i telefoni cellulari.

Did you have a good night?
Hai passato una bella serata?

a drink **un drink**	festival **il festival**	to see a show **vedere uno spettacolo**
nightlife **la vita notturna**	box office **la biglietteria**	to watch a film **guardare un film**
party **la festa**	to socialize **socializzare**	to go dancing **andare a ballare**
show **lo spettacolo**	to order food/drinks **ordinare da mangiare / da bere**	to enjoy oneself **divertirsi**
film **il film**		

YOU SHOULD KNOW...

Many bars and restaurants in Italian towns and cities have outdoor areas ideal for people-watching. Order a coffee or an "aperitivo", sit back, and relax.

ballet
la danza classica

bar
il locale

carnival
il carnevale

casino
il casinò

cinema
il cinema

comedy show
lo spettacolo comico

concert
il concerto

funfair
il luna park

musical
il musical

nightclub
il night

opera
l'opera *f*

restaurant
il ristorante

theatre
il teatro

Italy is one of the world's most visited countries, and there's a vast range of accommodation available for visitors, from high-end hotels to "pensioni" (guesthouses) and cosy bed and breakfasts. "Agriturismo" (a farm stay on or near a working farm) is popular with visitors, as is accommodation in the countryside.

YOU MIGHT SAY...

Have you got rooms available?
Avete camere disponibili?

How much is it per night?
Quant'è per notte?

Is breakfast included?
La colazione è inclusa?

Is there a city tax?
C'è una tassa di soggiorno?

I'd like to check in/out, please.
Vorrei fare il check in / out, per favore.

I have a reservation.
Ho una prenotazione.

I'd like to book a single/double room, please.
Vorrei prenotare una camera singola / doppia, per favore.

What time is breakfast served?
A che ora servite la colazione?

What time do I have to check out?
A che ora dovrei fare il check out?

Could I upgrade my room?
Potrei essere trasferito a una camera di categoria superiore?

I need fresh towels/more soap for my room.
Avrei bisogno di asciugamani puliti / più sapone.

I've lost my key.
Ho perduto la chiave.

I'd like to make a complaint.
Vorrei fare un reclamo.

I'm in room number...
Sono nella stanza numero...

YOU SHOULD KNOW...

When checking in to your hotel, you will be expected to fill out a registration form and provide your passport number.

YOU MIGHT HEAR...

We have/don't have rooms available.
Abbiamo / Non abbiamo camere disponibili.

Our rates are...
Le nostre tariffe sono...

Breakfast is/is not included.
La colazione è / non è inclusa.

Breakfast is served at...
Serviamo la colazione alle...

May I have your room number, please?
Potrei avere il numero della sua stanza, per favore?

May I see your documents, please?
Potrei vedere i suoi documenti, per favore?

You may check in after...
Può fare il check in dopo...

You must check out before...
Deve fare il check out prima...

VOCABULARY

bed and breakfast
il bed and breakfast

full board
la pensione completa

half board
la mezza pensione

room service
il servizio in camera

wake-up call
la sveglia

room number
il numero di camera

per person per night
per persona per notte

to check in
fare il check in

to check out
fare il check out

to order room service
ordinare il servizio in camera

corridor
il corridoio

"do not disturb" sign
il cartellino "non disturbare"

double room
la camera doppia

150

key card
la tessera magnetica

minibar
il minibar

porter
il facchino

reception
la reception

receptionist
il receptionist

safe
la cassaforte

single room
la camera singola

toiletries
gli articoli da toilette

twin room
la camera doppia con letti singoli

151

There are many campsites across Italy. While wild camping is generally forbidden, local regulations permit it in some places.

YOU MIGHT SAY...

Have you got spaces available?
Ci sono spazi disponibili?

I'd like to book for... nights.
Vorrei prenotare per ... notti.

How much is it per night?
Quant'è per notte?

Where is the toilet/shower block?
Dove sono i servizi igienici?

Is the water drinkable?
L'acqua è potabile?

Is it OK to camp here?
Ci si può accampare qui?

YOU MIGHT HEAR...

We don't have any spaces available.
Non abbiamo spazi disponibili.

It costs ... per night.
Costa ... per notte.

The toilets/showers are located...
I servizi igienici sono....

The water is/is not drinkable.
L'acqua è / non è potabile.

You can't put your tent up here.
Non può piantare la sua tenda qui.

VOCABULARY

campsite il campeggio	toilet/shower block i servizi igienici	to camp accamparsi
pitch il campo	camper il campeggiatore / la campeggiatrice	to pitch a tent montare una tenda
electricity hook-up il cavo di allacciamento elettrico	caravanner il roulottista	to take down a tent smontare una tenda
		to go caravanning andare in roulotte

YOU SHOULD KNOW...

If you plan on caravanning in Italy, be aware that taking a caravan or large camper van on the "autostrada" (motorway) will incur extra toll charges.

air bed
il materassino

barbecue
la griglia

camping stove
il fornello da
campeggio

caravan
il caravan

cool box
il frigo portatile

fold-up chair
la sedia pieghevole

matches
i fiammiferi

motorhome
il camper

picnic blanket
la coperta da picnic

sleeping bag
il sacco a pelo

tent
la tenda

torch
la torcia

Italy has over 7,500 kilometres of varying coastline, from rocky cliffs to fine sandy beaches. Most beaches are privately owned and charge a fee for use of the beach, as well as for umbrellas and sunbeds. There are also free beaches ("spiagge libere"), but these may not be as clean as private ones.

YOU MIGHT SAY...

Is there a good beach nearby?
C'è una bella spiaggia nelle vicinanze?

Is swimming permitted here?
È permessa la balneazione qui?

Is the water cold?
L'acqua è fredda?

Can we hire...?
Possiamo noleggiare...?

Help! Lifeguard!
Aiuto! Bagnino!

YOU MIGHT HEAR...

This is a public/private beach.
Questa è una spiaggia pubblica / privata.

Swimming is allowed/forbidden.
La balneazione è permessa / proibita.

Swimming is/is not supervised.
La balneazione è / non è sorvegliata.

The water is warm/cold/freezing!
L'acqua è calda / fredda / gelata!

VOCABULARY

"No swimming."
"Divieto di balneazione."

bathing zone
la zona di balneazione

lifeguard station
la postazione del bagnino

suntan
l'abbronzatura f

to sunbathe
prendere il sole

to swim
nuotare

YOU SHOULD KNOW...

Supervised beaches have a flag system to indicate bathing conditions.
Green – "safe to swim"
Yellow – "swim with caution"
Red – "dangerous for swimming".
Double red – "swimming forbidden and unmonitored".

THE SEASIDE

sand
la sabbia

sea
il mare

waves
le onde

parasol
l'ombrellone *m*

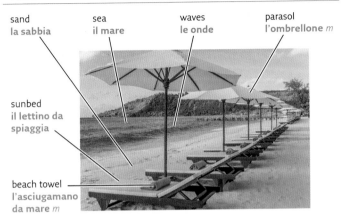

sunbed
il lettino da
spiaggia

beach towel
l'asciugamano
da mare *m*

GENERAL

beach ball
il pallone da
spiaggia

beach hut
la cabina da spiaggia

bikini
il bikini

bucket and spade
il secchiello e la
paletta

deckchair
la sdraio

flip-flops
le ciabatte infradito

flippers
le pinne

promenade
il lungomare

sandcastle
il castello di sabbia

seashells
le conchiglie

seaweed
l'alga marina *f*

snorkel
il boccaglio

sunglasses
gli occhiali da sole

sunhat
il cappello da sole

suntan lotion
la crema solare

swimming trunks
il costume da bagno

swimsuit
il costume da bagno

windbreak
il paravento

YOU MIGHT SAY...

I enjoy listening to music.
Mi piace ascoltare la musica.

What kind of music do you like?
Che tipo di musica ti piace?

I play...
Suono...

Is there a live music scene here?
C'è musica dal vivo in questa zona?

I'm learning to play...
Sto imparando a suonare...

YOU MIGHT HEAR...

I like/don't like...
Mi piace / Non mi piace...

There's a good music scene here.
C'è un buon panorama musicale qui.

My favourite group is...
Il mio gruppo preferito è...

VOCABULARY

DJ
il DJ

live music
la musica dal vivo

folk music
la musica popolare

CD
il CD

gig
il concerto

to play an instrument
suonare uno strumento

vinyl record
il disco in vinile

pop
il pop

to sing
cantare

microphone
il microfono

rock
il rock

to listen to music
ascoltare la musica

song
la canzone

hip-hop
la musica hip-hop

to go to gigs
andare ai concerti

band
il gruppo

rap
il rap

to stream music
ascoltare musica in streaming

singer-songwriter
il cantautore

classical music
la musica classica

157

Bluetooth® speaker
l'altoparlante
Bluetooth® *m*

earphones
gli auricolari

headphones
le cuffie

soundbar
il sistema SoundBar

speakers
gli altoparlanti

turntable
il giradischi

MUSICAL INSTRUMENTS

accordion
la fisarmonica

acoustic guitar
la chitarra acustica

bass drum
la grancassa

bass guitar
il basso

cello
il violoncello

clarinet
il clarinetto

double bass
il contrabbasso

cymbals
i piatti

electric guitar
la chitarra elettrica

flute
il flauto

harp
l'arpa *f*

keyboard
la tastiera

mouth organ
l'armonica a bocca *f*

piano
il pianoforte

saxophone
il sassofono

159

snare drum
il tamburo rullante

trombone
il trombone

trumpet
la tromba

tuba
la tuba

violin
il violino

xylophone
lo xilofono

GENERAL

choir
il coro

conductor
**il direttore
d'orchestra**

musician
**il musicista /
la musicista**

orchestra
l'orchestra *f*

sheet music
lo spartito

singer
**il cantante /
la cantante**

YOU MIGHT SAY...

Can I take photos here?
Si possono fare fotografie qui?

Where can I print my photos?
Dove posso stampare le mie foto?

YOU MIGHT HEAR...

Photography isn't allowed.
Non è permesso scattare fotografie.

Say cheese!
Di 'cheese'!

VOCABULARY

photographer il fotografo	close-up il primo piano	to take a photo/selfie fare una foto / un selfie
photo la foto	selfie il selfie	to upload a photo caricare una foto
photo album l'album di foto *m*	selfie stick il bastone per i selfie	to zoom in zumare

camera lens
la lente

compact camera
la macchina
fotografica compatta

drone
il drone

DSLR camera
la macchina
fotografica DSLR

SD card
la scheda SD

tripod
il treppiede

YOU MIGHT SAY...

Shall we play a game?
Facciamo un gioco?

What would you like to play?
A che vuoi giocare?

What are the rules?
Quali sono le regole?

YOU MIGHT HEAR...

It's your turn.
È il tuo turno.

Time's up!
Tempo scaduto.

Shall we play something else?
Giochiamo a qualcos'altro?

VOCABULARY

player il giocatore	hand (in cards) la mano	to play giocare
charades il gioco dei mimi	video game il videogioco	to roll the dice tirare i dadi
hide and seek il nascondino	games console la console	to win vincere
skittles i birilli	game controller il controller	to lose perdere
solitaire il solitario	joystick il joystick	to play tag giocare ad acchiapparella
poker il poker	virtual reality headset il visore per la realtà virtuale	

YOU SHOULD KNOW...

As an alternative to playing games in the evening, the evening stroll or "passeggiata" takes place in towns, cities, and villages across Italy. As dusk descends, Italians emerge to stroll through pedestrian areas or along the seafront, to enjoy the evening air, to see and be seen, to chat, and maybe to sip an "aperitivo" at a table on the pavement.

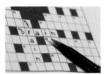

backgammon
il tric-trac

board game
il gioco da tavolo

bowling
il bowling

cards
le carte

chess
gli scacchi

counters
i segnalini

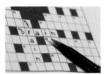

crossword
il cruciverba

darts
le freccette

dice
i dadi

dominoes
il domino

draughts
la dama

jigsaw puzzle
il puzzle

163

Italy offers a wide range of themed activity holidays, from cycling and hiking to yoga, arts and crafts, cookery and painting.

VOCABULARY

handicrafts **l'artigianato** *m*	artist **l'artista** *m*	to sketch **fare uno schizzo**
craft fair **la fiera dell'artigianato**	dressmaker **il sarto / la sarta**	to sew **cucire**
cardboard **il cartone**	amateur **dilettante**	to knit **fare la maglia**
glue **la colla**	to paint **dipingere**	to be creative **essere creativo**

GENERAL CRAFTS

collage
il collage

embroidery
il ricamo

jewellery-making
la gioielleria

model-making
il modellismo

pottery
la ceramica

woodwork
la carpenteria

canvas
la tela

easel
il cavalletto

ink
l'inchiostro *m*

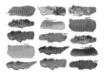

oil paint
la pittura a olio

paintbrush
il pennello

palette
la tavolozza

paper
la carta

pastels
i pastelli

pen
la penna

pencil
la matita

sketchpad
l'album per schizzi *m*

watercolours
gli acquerelli

ball of wool
il gomitolo di lana

buttons
i bottoni

crochet hook
l'uncinetto *m*

fabric
il tessuto

fabric scissors
le forbici da tessuto

knitting needles
i ferri da maglia

needle and thread
l'ago e il filo *m*

pins
gli spilli

safety pin
la spilla da balia

sewing basket
il cestino del cucito

sewing machine
la macchina da
cucire

tape measure
il metro a nastro

SPORT | LO SPORT

Be it football or rugby, cycling or skiing, Italy has a long sporting history. There are hundreds of sports and fitness clubs, plus events across the country that you can get involved with, either as a player or as a spectator. You may wish to participate in a sport, head to the gym, or simply chat about how "gli Azzurri" are getting on.

football pitch
il campo da calcio

centre circle
il cerchio di centrocampo

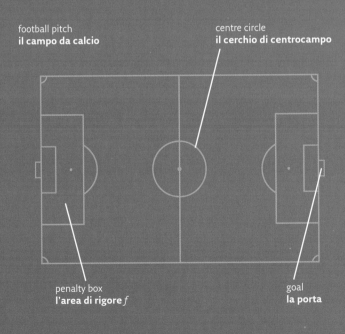

penalty box
l'area di rigore *f*

goal
la porta

YOU MIGHT SAY...

I like keeping active.
Mi piace essere attivo.

Where is...?
Dov'è...?

Where is the nearest...?
Dov'è il ... più vicino?

I train ... times per week.
Mi alleno ... volte a settimana.

I play rugby/hockey.
Gioco a rugby / hockey.

I'd like to book...
Vorrei prenotare...

YOU MIGHT HEAR...

There's a ... nearby.
C'è un ... qui vicino.

Do you do any sports?
Fa sport?

Where/When do you train?
Dove / Quando si allena?

Do you follow any sports?
Segue qualche sport?

What's your favourite team?
Qual'è la sua squadra preferita?

I'm a fan of...
Sono un fan di...

VOCABULARY

tournament
il torneo

competition
la competizione

league
la lega

champion
**il campione /
la campionessa**

competitor
**il concorrente /
la concorrente**

teammate
**il compagno di
squadra /
la compagna di
squadra**

coach
l'allenatore *m* **/
l'allenatrice** *f*

manager
il manager

match
la partita

points
i punti

to coach
allenare

to compete
competere

to score
segnare

to win
vincere

to lose
perdere

to draw
pareggiare

leisure centre
il centro sportivo

medal
la medaglia

official
l'arbitro *m*

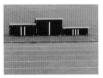
podium
il podio

referee
l'arbitro *m*

scoreboard
**il tabellone
segnapunti**

spectators
gli spettatori

sportsperson
**lo sportivo /
la sportiva**

stadium
lo stadio

stands
le tribune

team
la squadra sportiva

trophy
il trofeo

YOU MIGHT SAY...

I'd like to join the gym.
Vorrei iscrivermi in palestra.

I'd like to book a class.
Vorrei prenotare una lezione.

What are the facilities like?
Come sono gli attrezzi?

What kinds of classes can you do here?
Che tipo di lezioni fate qui?

YOU MIGHT HEAR...

Are you a member here?
È socio qui?

Would you like to book an induction?
Vuole prenotare una lezione di prova?

What time would you like to book for?
Per che ora vuole prenotare?

VOCABULARY

gym **la palestra**	Pilates **il Pilates**	walking **il camminare**
gym membership **l'iscrizione in palestra** *m*	yoga **lo yoga**	to exercise **fare esercizio**
personal trainer **il personal trainer**	press-ups **le flessioni**	to keep fit **mantenersi in forma**
exercise class **la lezione di ginnastica**	sit-ups **gli addominali** running **la corsa**	to go for a run **andare a correre** to go to the gym **andare in palestra**

YOU SHOULD KNOW...

Be aware of membership and cancellation conditions: some gyms may expect you to continue paying for the duration of your membership even if you are unable to continue attending the gym, so it's best to check the fine print carefully.

changing room
lo spogliatoio

cross trainer
il cross trainer

dumbbells
i manubri

exercise bike
la cyclette

gym ball
la palla da ginnastica

kettle bell
il kettlebell

locker
l'armadietto m

rowing machine
il vogatore

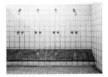

showers
le docce

skipping rope
la corda

treadmill
il tapis roulant

weightlifting bench
la panca

Football is the most widely played sport in Italy. The national team have been World Cup and European winners.

YOU MIGHT SAY...

Are you going to watch the match?
Pensa di guardare la partita?

What's the score?
Qual è il punteggio?

That was a foul!
Quello è un fallo!

YOU MIGHT HEAR...

I'm watching the match.
Sto guardando la partita.

The score is...
Il punteggio è...

Go on!
Vai!

VOCABULARY

defender
il difensore

striker
l'attaccante *m*

substitute
la riserva

kick-off
il calcio d'inizio

half-time
l'intervallo *m*

full-time
la fine della partita

extra time
**i tempi
supplementari**

injury time
i minuti di recupero

free kick
il calcio di punizione

header
il colpo di testa

save
la parata

foul
il rigore

tackle
il contrasto

offside
il fuori gioco

penalty kick
il calcio di rigore

penalty box
l'area di rigore *f*

to play football
giocare a calcio

to kick
calciare

to tackle
contrastare

to pass the ball
passare la palla

to score a goal
fare gol

assistant referee
il guardalinee

football
il pallone da calcio

football boots
gli scarpini da calcio

football match
la partita di calcio

football pitch
il campo da calcio

football player
il calciatore

goal
la porta

goalkeeper
il portiere

goalkeeper's gloves
i guanti da portiere

shin pads
i parastinchi

whistle
il fischietto

yellow/red card
il cartellino giallo / rosso

Italy has played international rugby union since 1929 but the sport has become much more popular since Italy joined the Five Nations Championship (making it the Six Nations) in 2000. The national teams are called "gli Azzurri", like the football team.

VOCABULARY

rugby league/union
il rugby a tredici / quindici

forward
l'avanti *m*

back
il tre quarti

try
la meta

conversion
la trasformazione

penalty kick
il calcio di rigore

drop goal
il goal di rimbalzo

tackle
il placcaggio

pass
il passaggio

to play rugby
giocare a rugby

to tackle
placcare

to score a try
segnare una meta

rugby
il rugby

rugby ball
il pallone da rugby

rugby field
il campo di rugby

(rugby) goalposts
i pali di porta

rugby player
il rugbista

scrum
la mischia

Italy has one of the longest basketball-playing traditions in the world, and Italian teams do well in international competitions. A number of Italian basketball players have played in the American NBA.

VOCABULARY

wheelchair basketball **la pallacanestro in carrozzina**	to play basketball **giocare a pallacanestro**	to dribble **palleggiare**
slam dunk **la schiacciata**	to catch **prendere**	to block **bloccare**
free throw **il tiro libero**	to throw **tirare**	to mark a player **marcare un giocatore**

basket
il canestro

basketball
la palla da pallacanestro

basketball court
il campo da pallacanestro

basketball game
la partita di pallacanestro

basketball player
il giocatore di pallacanestro

basketball shoes
le scarpe da pallacanestro

VOCABULARY

ace **l'ace** m	net **la rete**	to play tennis **giocare a tennis**
serve **il servizio**	rally **il palleggio**	to play badminton **giocare a badminton**
backhand **il rovescio**	singles **il singolo**	to hit **colpire**
forehand **il dritto**	doubles **il doppio**	to serve **servire**
fault **il fallo**	top seed **il numero uno**	to break someone's serve **strappare il servizio**

BADMINTON

badminton
il badminton

badminton racket
la racchetta da badminton

shuttlecock
il volano

SQUASH

squash
lo squash

squash ball
la pallina da squash

squash racket
la racchetta da squash

ball boy/girl
**il raccattapalle /
la raccattapalle**

line judge
il giudice di linea

tennis
il tennis

tennis ball
la pallina da tennis

tennis court
il campo da tennis

tennis player
il tennista

tennis racket
**la racchetta da
tennis**

umpire
l'arbitro *m*

umpire's chair
la sedia dell'arbitro

WATER SPORTS | GLI SPORT ACQUATICI

There are a whole range of water sports you can try out whilst in Italy, by the coast as well as inland. It's always advisable to seek out experienced instructors and source any appropriate safety equipment.

YOU MIGHT SAY...

I'm a keen swimmer.
Sono un appassionato di nuoto.

I'm not a strong swimmer.
Non sono un gran nuotatore.

Can I hire...?
Posso affittare...

YOU MIGHT HEAR...

The pool is...
La piscina è...

You can hire...
Può affittare...

You must wear a lifejacket.
Deve indossare un giubbotto di salvataggio.

VOCABULARY

swimming
il nuoto

breaststroke
la rana

backstroke
il dorso

front crawl
lo stile libero

butterfly
il delfino

lane
la corsia

length
la vasca

swimming lesson
la lezione di nuoto

swimmer
**il nuotatore /
la nuotatrice**

diver
il tuffatore

diving
il tuffo

angling
la pesca

angler
il pescatore

surfer
**il surfista /
la surfista**

to swim
nuotare

to dive
tuffarsi

to surf
fare surf

to paddle
pagaiare

to row
remare

to fish
pescare

to sail
navigare

armbands
i braccioli

diving board
il trampolino

flippers
le pinne

goggles
gli occhialini

lifeguard
**il bagnino /
la bagnina**

swimming cap
la cuffia

swimming pool
la piscina

swimming trunks
il costume da bagno

swimsuit
il costume da bagno

OPEN WATER

bodyboarding
il bodyboard

canoeing
andare in canoa

jet ski
la moto d'acqua

179

kayaking
andare in kayak

lifejacket
il giubbotto di salvataggio

oars
i remi

paddle
la pagaia

paddleboarding
il paddle

scuba diving
l'immersione subacquea *f*

snorkelling
lo snorkelling

surfboard
la tavola da surf

surfing
il fare surf

waterskiing
lo sci d'acqua

wetsuit
la muta

windsurfing
il windsurf

With the Alps running across the north of the country, and the Apennines down the centre, there are plenty of opportunities to try mountain and winter sports in Italy.

YOU MIGHT SAY...

Can I hire some skis?
Posso noleggiare degli sci?

I'd like a skiing lesson, please.
Vorrei fare una lezione di sci.

I can't ski very well.
Non so sciare molto bene.

What are the snow conditions like?
Come sono le condizioni per sciare?

I've fallen.
Sono caduto.

I've hurt myself.
Mi sono fatto male.

Help!
Aiuto!

YOU MIGHT HEAR...

You can hire skis here.
Può noleggiare gli sci qui.

You can book a skiing lesson here.
Può prenotare una lezione di sci qui.

Do you have much skiing experience?
Ha molta esperienza come sciatore?

The piste is open/closed today.
La pista è aperta / chiusa oggi.

The conditions are good/bad.
Le condizioni sono buone / cattive.

There's an avalanche risk.
C'è il rischio di valanghe.

Be careful.
Stia attento.

VOCABULARY

skier
lo sciatore / la sciatrice

ski resort
la stazione sciistica

ski lift
l'impianto di risalita *m*

ski instructor
l'istruttore di sci *m* / **l'istruttrice di sci** *f*

skiing lesson
la lezione di sci

mountain rescue service
il servizio di soccorso alpino

first-aid kit **il kit di pronto soccorso**	avalanche **la valanga**	to snowboard **fare snowboard**
snow **la neve**	avalanche warning **l'avviso di valanghe** *m*	to go mountain climbing **fare alpinismo**
powder **la neve farinosa**	carabiner clip **il moschettone**	to go sledging **andare in slitta**
ice **il ghiaccio**	to ski (off-piste) **sciare (fuori pista)**	to go skating **andare a pattinare**

YOU SHOULD KNOW...

Whilst there are relatively few restrictions on where you can ski in the Italian mountains, it's a good idea to have a guide accompany you if you do wish to try an off-piste route. Cross-country skiing ("sci di fondo') is also a very popular winter activity.

GENERAL

crampons
i ramponi

ice axe
la piccozza da ghiaccio

ice skates
i pattini da ghiaccio

ice skating
il pattinaggio su ghiaccio

rope
la cima

sledge
la slitta

piste
la pista

salopettes
la salopette

ski boots
gli scarponi da sci

ski gloves
i guanti da sci

ski goggles
la maschera da sci

ski helmet
il casco da sci

ski jacket
la giacca da sci

ski poles
i bastoncini da sci

skis
gli sci

ski suit
la tuta da sci

snowboard
lo snowboard

snowboarding boots
**gli scarponi da
snowboard**

VOCABULARY

fight **la lotta**	punch **il pugno**	to punch **dare un pugno**
boxer **il pugile**	knockout **il fuori combattimento**	to kick **dare un calcio**
fighter **il lottatore**	martial arts **le arti marziali**	to strike **colpire**
opponent **l'avversario** *m*	to box **fare il pugilato**	to spar **allenarsi**
featherweight **il peso piuma**	to wrestle **fare wrestling**	to knock out **mettere fuori combattimento**
heavyweight **il peso massimo**		

BOXING

boxing gloves
i guanti da boxe

boxing ring
il ring

boxing shoes
le scarpe da boxe

headguard
il paratesta

mouthguard
il paradenti

punchbag
il sacco da boxe

fencing
la scherma

judo
il judo

karate
il karatè

kickboxing
il kickboxing

tai chi
il tai chi

wrestling
il wrestling

taekwondo
il taekwondo

VOCABULARY

runner **il corridore**	finish line **la linea di arrivo**	starter's gun **il colpo di partenza**
race **la gara**	heat **la batteria**	to do athletics **fare atletica**
marathon **la maratona**	final **la finale**	to run **correre**
sprint **lo sprint**	triple jump **il salto triplo**	to race **gareggiare**
lane **la corsia**	heptathlon **l'eptathlon** *m*	to jump **saltare**
start line **la linea di partenza**	decathlon **il decathlon**	to throw **tirare**

athlete
l'atleta *m* / **l'atleta** *f*

discus
il disco

high jump
il salto in alto

hurdles
gli ostacoli

javelin
il giavellotto

long jump
il salto in lungo

pole vault
il salto con l'asta

relay
la staffetta

running track
la pista da corsa

shot put
il lancio del peso

starting blocks
i blocchi di partenza

stopwatch
il cronometro

spikes
le scarpette chiodate

There are golf courses and clubs in many parts of Italy. Golfing holidays are becoming increasingly popular, and you can hire any equipment you may need.

VOCABULARY

golfer
**il giocatore di golf /
la giocatrice di golf**

caddie
il portabastoni

golf course
il campo da golf

fairway
il fairway

green
il green

bunker
il bunker

hole
la buca

clubhouse
il clubhouse

hole-in-one
la buca in uno

birdie
il birdie

bogey
il bogey

handicap
l'handicap *m*

over/under par
sopra / sotto il par

to play golf
giocare a golf

to tee off
**lanciare la palla dal
tee**

golf bag
la borsa da golf

golf ball
la pallina da golf

golf buggy
la golf car

golf club
il bastone da golf

putter
il putter

tee
il tee

American football
il football americano

archery
il tiro con l'arco

baseball
il baseball

bowls
le bocce

climbing
l'arrampicata *f*

cricket
il cricket

fishing
la pesca

gymnastics
la ginnastica artistica

handball
la pallamano

hockey
l'hockey *m*

horse racing
l'ippica *f*

ice hockey
l'hockey sul ghiaccio *m*

motorcycle racing
il motociclismo

motor racing
le gare automobilistiche

netball
il netball

shooting
il tiro al bersaglio

showjumping
il concorso ippico

skateboarding
lo skateboard

snooker
lo snooker

table tennis
il ping pong

track cycling
il ciclismo su pista

volleyball
la pallavolo

water polo
la pallanuoto

weightlifting
il sollevamento pesi

Italy's national public health service ("Servizio Sanitario Nazionale") is free at the point of use for citizens and residents, and private medical care is also available. It's important to arrange appropriate cover for healthcare during your time in Italy. If you are a holidaymaker, ensure you have appropriate travel insurance in place.

first-aid kit
il kit di pronto soccorso

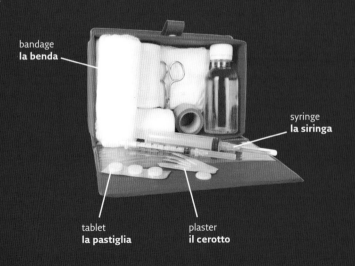

bandage
la benda

syringe
la siringa

tablet
la pastiglia

plaster
il cerotto

The pharmacy is usually the first port of call for most minor ailments, especially since smaller villages or more remote areas may not be served by a doctor's surgery. 112 is the Universal European Emergency Services phone number, used for all emergency services in Italy. It works from all phones, including mobiles, and will connect you to the appropriate emergency service.

YOU MIGHT SAY...

I don't feel well.
Non mi sento bene.

He/She doesn't feel well.
Non si sente bene.

I'm going to be sick.
Sto per vomitare.

I need to see a doctor.
Ho bisogno di un dottore.

I need to go to hospital.
Ho bisogno di andare all'ospedale.

Call an ambulance.
Chiami un'ambulanza.

YOU MIGHT HEAR...

What's wrong?
Cosa c'è che non va?

Where does it hurt?
Dove le fa male?

What happened?
Cos'è successo?

How long have you been feeling ill?
Da quanto tempo si sente male?

YOU SHOULD KNOW...

The Italian Health Insurance card ("Tessera Sanitaria") is the national social security card, which contains personal data about the holder as well as their tax code. If you are staying in Italy for more than 90 days you need to register with the health service ("Servizio Sanitario Nazionale") at your local health centre ("Azienda Sanitaria Locale" or "ASL").

VOCABULARY

first aider **il soccorritore / la soccorritrice**	pain **il dolore**	illness **la malattia**

mental health
la sanità mentale

health insurance
**l'assicurazione
sanitaria** *f*

to recover
guarire

treatment
la terapia

healthy
sano

to look after
occuparsi di

recovery
la guarigione

to be unwell
stare male

to treat
curare

doctor
**il dottore /
la dottoressa**

first-aid kit
**il kit di pronto
soccorso**

hospital
l'ospedale *m*

medicine
la medicina

nurse
l'infermiere *m* /
l'infermiera *f*

paramedic
il paramedico

patient
**il paziente /
la paziente**

pharmacist
**il farmacista /
la farmacista**

pharmacy
la farmacia

VOCABULARY

throat **la gola**	tongue **la lingua**	sense of touch **il tatto**
armpit **l'ascella** *f*	skin **la pelle**	balance **l'equilibrio** *m*
genitals **i genitali**	(body) hair **i peli**	to see **vedere**
breast **il seno**	height **l'altezza** *f*	to smell **odorare**
eyelash **la ciglia**	weight **il peso**	to hear **ascoltare**
eyebrow **il sopracciglio**	BMI **l'indice di massa corporea** *m*	to touch **toccare**
eyelid **la palpebra**	sense of hearing **l'udito** *m*	to taste **assaggiare**
earlobe **il lobo dell'orecchio**	sense of sight **la vista**	to stand **stare in piedi**
nostrils **le narici**	sense of smell **l'olfatto** *m*	to walk **camminare**
lips **le labbra**	sense of taste **il gusto**	to lose one's balance **perdere l'equilibrio**

YOU SHOULD KNOW...

In Italian, possessive adjectives are not used to refer to one's body parts.
You use a reflexive verb instead, so that, for instance, "I washed my hands"
is translated as "Mi sono lavata le mani".

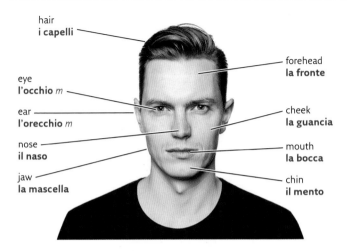

hair
i capelli

forehead
la fronte

eye
l'occhio *m*

ear
l'orecchio *m*

cheek
la guancia

nose
il naso

mouth
la bocca

jaw
la mascella

chin
il mento

HAND

FOOT

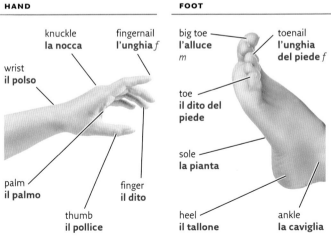

knuckle
la nocca

fingernail
l'unghia *f*

wrist
il polso

big toe
l'alluce
m

toenail
**l'unghia
del piede** *f*

toe
**il dito del
piede**

sole
la pianta

palm
il palmo

finger
il dito

thumb
il pollice

heel
il tallone

ankle
la caviglia

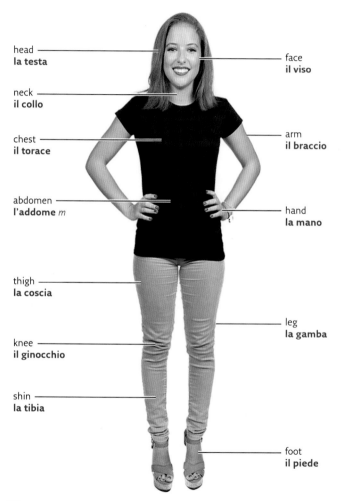

head
la testa

face
il viso

neck
il collo

chest
il torace

arm
il braccio

abdomen
l'addome *m*

hand
la mano

thigh
la coscia

leg
la gamba

knee
il ginocchio

shin
la tibia

foot
il piede

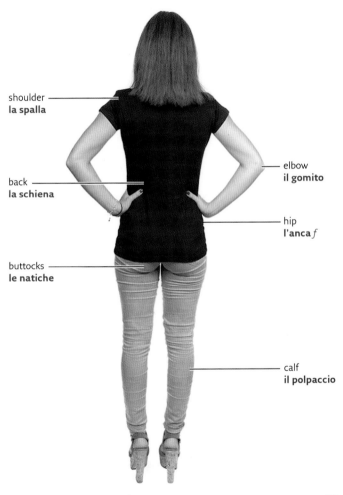

shoulder
la spalla

back
la schiena

buttocks
le natiche

elbow
il gomito

hip
l'anca *f*

calf
il polpaccio

Hopefully this is not vocabulary you will need very often, but it is useful to have the necessary terminology at your disposal should the need arise.

VOCABULARY

organ
l'organo *m*

brain
il cervello

heart
il cuore

lung
il polmone

liver
il fegato

stomach
lo stomaco

kidney
il rene

intestines
l'intestino *m*

digestive system
l'apparato digerente *m*

respiratory system
l'apparato respiratorio *m*

bladder
la vescica

blood
il sangue

joint
l'articolazione *f*

bone
l'osso *m*

muscle
il muscolo

tendon
il tendine

ligament
il legamento

tissue
il tessuto

cell
la cellula

artery
l'arteria *f*

vein
la vena

oxygen
l'ossigeno *m*

YOU SHOULD KNOW...

Parts of the body feature often in common Italian expressions, such as:
"acqua in bocca" meaning "to keep quiet" (literally: water in your mouth)
"farsi mettere i piedi in testa" meaning "to let someone walk all over you" (literally: to let someone put their feet on your head)
"avere le mani bucate" meaning "to be a spendthrift" (literally: to have holes in your hands).

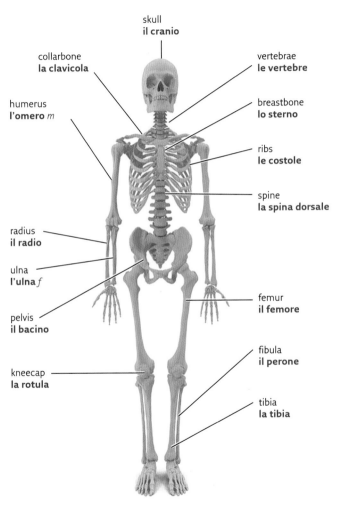

skull
il cranio

collarbone
la clavicola

vertebrae
le vertebre

humerus
l'omero *m*

breastbone
lo sterno

ribs
le costole

spine
la spina dorsale

radius
il radio

ulna
l'ulna *f*

pelvis
il bacino

femur
il femore

fibula
il perone

kneecap
la rotula

tibia
la tibia

When attending a doctor's appointment, you will need to show some form of ID.

YOU MIGHT SAY...

I'd like to make an appointment.
Vorrei prendere un appuntamento.

That hurts.
Fa male.

I have an appointment with Dr...
Ho un appuntamento con il dottor...

I'm allergic to...
Sono allergico/a a...

I take medication for...
Prendo farmaci per...

I've been feeling unwell.
Non mi sento bene.

YOU MIGHT HEAR...

Your appointment is at...
Il suo appuntamento è alle...

The doctor will call you through.
Il dottore la chiamerà.

What are your symptoms?
Quali sono i suoi sintomi?

May I examine you?
Posso visitarla?

Tell me if that hurts.
Mi dica se fa male.

Do you have any allergies?
Ha allergie?

Do you take any medication?
Prende dei farmaci?

Take two tablets twice a day.
Prenda due pasticche due volte al giorno.

You need to see a specialist.
Ha bisogno di consultare uno specialista.

VOCABULARY

appointment
l'appuntamento *m*

clinic
la clinica

examination
l'analisi *f*

test
l'esame *m*

prescription
la ricetta

to make an
appointment
**prendere un
appuntamento**

antibiotics
gli antibiotici

home visit
la visita a domicilio

the pill
la pillola

vaccination
la vaccinazione

to examine
visitare

sleeping pill
il sonnifero

medication
il medicinale

to be on medication
prendere medicine

blood pressure monitor
**il misuratore di
pressione sanguigna**

examination room
l'ambulatorio *m*

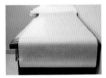

examination table
il lettino

GP
il medico di base

practice nurse
l'infermiere *m* /
l'infermiera *f*

stethoscope
lo stetoscopio

syringe
la siringa

thermometer
il termometro

waiting room
la sala d'attesa

YOU MIGHT SAY...

Can I book an emergency appointment?
Potrei prenotare un appuntamento d'emergenza?

I have toothache.
Ho il mal di denti.

I have an abscess.
Ho un ascesso.

My filling has come out.
L'otturazione si è tolta.

I've broken my tooth.
Mi si è rotto un dente.

My dentures are broken.
La mia dentiera si è rotta.

YOU MIGHT HEAR...

We don't have any emergency appointments available.
Non abbiamo appuntamenti d'emergenza disponibili.

You need a new filling.
Ha bisogno di una nuova otturazione.

Your tooth has to come out.
Il dente deve essere tolto.

You will need to make another appointment.
Deve prendere un altro appuntamento.

VOCABULARY

dental check-up
il controllo dei denti

hygienist
l'igienista m /
l'igienista f

molar
il molare

incisor
l'incisivo m

canine
il canino

wisdom teeth
i denti del giudizio

filling
l'otturazione f

crown
la corona dentale

root canal treatment
la cura canalare

toothache
il mal di denti

abscess
l'ascesso m

extraction
l'estrazione f

to brush one's teeth
lavarsi i denti

to floss
usare il filo interdentale

braces
l'apparecchio *m*

dental floss
il filo interdentale

dental nurse
l'assistente dentale *m* /
l'assistente dentale *f*

dentist
il dentista

dentist's chair
il lettino da dentista

dentist's drill
**il trapano da
dentista**

dentures
la dentiera

gums
le gengive

mouthwash
il collutorio

teeth
i denti

toothbrush
**lo spazzolino da
denti**

toothpaste
il dentifricio

Eye tests in Italy are not usually carried out by opticians, but by ophthalmologists, who can provide you with a prescription for glasses to take to an optician.

YOU MIGHT SAY...

Can I book an appointment?
Posso prenotare un appuntamento?

My eyes are dry.
Ho gli occhi asciutti.

My eyes are sore.
Mi fanno male gli occhi.

Do you repair glasses?
Riparate gli occhiali?

YOU MIGHT HEAR...

Your appointment is at...
Il suo appuntamento è alle...

Look up/down/ahead.
Guardi su / giù / dritto.

Read the letters on the first/second row.
Legga le lettere della prima / seconda linea.

VOCABULARY

ophthalmologist
l'oftalmologo *m*

reading glasses
gli occhiali da lettura

bifocals
i bifocali

hard/soft contact lenses
le lenti a contatto rigide / morbide

lens
la lente

conjunctivitis
la congiuntivite

stye
l'orzaiolo *m*

blurred vision
la vista sfocata

cataract
la cataratta

short-sighted
miope

long-sighted
presbite

visually impaired
ipovedente

blind
non vedente

colour-blind
daltonico

to wear glasses
portare gli occhiali

to wear contacts
portare le lenti a contatto

contact lenses
le lenti a contatto

contact lens case
il contenitore per le lenti a contatto

eye chart
la tabella di misurazione della vista

eye drops
il collirio

eye test
l'esame della vista *m*

frames
la montatura

glasses
gli occhiali

glasses case
la custodia per gli occhiali

optician
l'ottico *m*

There are both public hospitals ("ospedali") and private hospitals ("case di cura" or "cliniche") available in Italy. Private hospitals tend to specialize in particular fields of medicine and do not have accident and emergency departments.

YOU MIGHT SAY...

Which ward is ... in?
In che reparto è...?

When are visiting hours?
Qual'è l'orario di visita?

YOU MIGHT HEAR...

He/She is in ward...
È nel reparto...

Visiting hours are between ... and...
L'orario di visita è dalle ... alle...

VOCABULARY

public hospital
l'ospedale pubblico *m*

private hospital
l'ospedale privato *m*

physiotherapist
**il fisioterapista /
la fisioterapista**

radiographer
**il radiografo /
la radiografa**

surgeon
il chirurgo

operation
l'operazione *f*

scan
l'ecografia *f*

intensive care
la terapia intensiva

defibrillator
il defibrillatore

diagnosis
la diagnosi

to undergo surgery
**sottoporsi a un
intervento chirurgico**

to be admitted
**essere ricoverato in
ospedale**

to be discharged
**essere dimesso
dall'ospedale**

A&E
il pronto soccorso

ambulance
l'ambulanza *f*

crutches
le stampelle

drip
la flebo

hospital bed
il letto d'ospedale

hospital trolley
il carrello ospedaliero

monitor
il monitor

operating theatre
la sala operatoria

oxygen mask
la maschera d'ossigeno

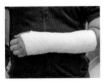

plaster cast
l'ingessatura *f*

stitches
i punti

ward
il reparto

wheelchair
la sedia a rotelle

X-ray
la radiografia

Zimmer frame®
il deambulatore

YOU MIGHT SAY...

Can you call an ambulance?
Può chiamare un'ambulanza?

I've had an accident.
Ho avuto un incidente.

I've hurt my...
Mi sono fatto male al / alla...

I've broken/sprained my...
Mi sono rotto / storto il / la...

I've cut/burnt myself.
Mi sono tagliato / bruciato.

I've hit my head.
Ho sbattuto la testa.

YOU MIGHT HEAR...

Do you feel sick/faint?
Si sente male / svenire?

I'm calling an ambulance.
Chiamo un'ambulanza.

Where does it hurt?
Dove le fa male?

Are you able to move it?
Riesce a muoverlo/a?

Tell me what happened.
Mi dica cos'è successo.

YOU SHOULD KNOW...

If a medical situation is not an emergency, a "guardia medica", or first-aid service, may be sent to give medical assistance.

VOCABULARY

pulse **il polso**	dislocation **la lussazione**	swelling **il gonfiore**
concussion **la commozione cerebrale**	sprain **la slogatura**	first aid **il pronto soccorso**
accident **l'incidente** m	scar **la cicatrice**	recovery position **la posizione di sicurezza**
fall **la caduta**	whiplash **il colpo di frusta**	CPR **la rianimazione**

to be unconscious	to fall	to twist one's ankle
essere svenuto	**cadere**	**slogarsi la caviglia**
to injure oneself	to break one's arm	to take his/her pulse
farsi male	**rompersi il braccio**	**sentire il polso**

INJURIES

blister
la vescica

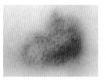

bruise
il livido

burn
la bruciatura

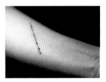

cut
il taglio

fracture
la frattura

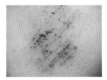

graze
l'escoriazione *f*

splinter
la scheggia

sting
la puntura

sunburn
la scottatura

antiseptic
l'antisettico *m*

bandage
la benda

dressing
la garza

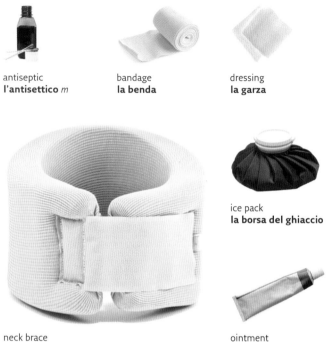

neck brace
il collare

ice pack
la borsa del ghiaccio

ointment
la pomata

plaster
il cerotto

sling
la fascia

tweezers
le pinzette

YOU MIGHT SAY...

I have a cold/the flu.
Ho il raffreddore / l'influenza.

I'm going to be sick.
Sto per vomitare.

I have a sore stomach.
Ho il mal di stomaco.

I'm asthmatic/diabetic.
Ho l'asma / il diabete.

YOU MIGHT HEAR...

You should go to the doctor.
Dovrebbe andare dal dottore.

You need to rest.
Ha bisogno di riposo.

VOCABULARY

heart attack
l'attacco cardiaco *m*

stroke
l'ictus *m*

infection
l'infezione *f*

ear infection
l'otite *f*

fever
la febbre

virus
il virus

chicken pox
la varicella

rash
l'eruzione cutanea *f*

stomach bug
il virus intestinale

food poisoning
l'intossicazione alimentare *f*

vomiting
il vomito

nausea
la nausea

diarrhoea
la diarrea

constipation
la stitichezza

diabetes
il diabete

epilepsy
l'epilessia *f*

asthma
l'asma *f*

dizziness
le vertigini

inhaler
l'inalatore *m*

insulin
l'insulina *f*

period pain
i dolori mestruali

to have high/low blood pressure
avere la pressione alta / bassa

to cough
tossire

to sneeze
starnutire

to vomit
vomitare

to faint
svenire

If you plan to have your baby in Italy, you will be referred to a gynaecologist who will be your principal contact during the pregnancy and who will give advice on maternity hospitals and midwives. Although maternity care is available on the Italian national health service, many women prefer to see a private gynaecologist.

YOU MIGHT SAY...

I'm (six months) pregnant.
Sono incinta (di sei mesi).

My partner/wife is pregnant.
La mia partner / mia moglie è incinta.

I'm/She's having contractions every ... minutes.
Ho / Ha contrazioni ogni ... minuti.

My/Her waters have broken.
Mi / Le si sono rotte le acque.

I need pain relief.
Ho bisogno di un antidolorifico.

YOU MIGHT HEAR...

How far along are you?
È incinta di quanti mesi?

How long is it between contractions?
Quanto tempo passa tra una contrazione e l'altra?

Push!
Spinga!

May I examine you?
Posso esaminarla?

VOCABULARY

pregnant woman
la donna incinta

newborn
il neonato

foetus
il feto

uterus
l'utero *m*

cervix
la cervice

pre-natal class
il corso preparto

labour
il travaglio

delivery
il parto

Caesarean section
il parto cesareo

epidural
l'anestesia epidurale *f*

miscarriage
l'aborto spontaneo *m*

stillborn
nato morto

to fall pregnant
rimanere incinta

to give birth
partorire

due date
la data del parto

to be overdue
essere oltre il termine

to miscarry
abortire

morning sickness
la nausea mattutina

to be in labour
avere le doglie

to breast-feed
allattare

baby blanket
la coperta per bambini

babygro®
la tutina

incubator
l'incubatrice *f*

labour suite
la sala parto

midwife
l'ostetrica *f*

nappy
il pannolino

pregnancy test
il test di gravidanza

sonographer
l'ecografista *m* /
l'ecografista *f*

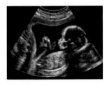

ultrasound
l'ecografia *f*

Alternative therapies are popular in Italy, but not all are eligible for social security cover, so it is worth researching which treatments can be covered by standard insurance.

VOCABULARY

therapist **il terapista**	acupuncturist **l'agopunturista** *m*	mindfulness **la consapevolezza**
masseur **il massaggiatore**	reflexologist **il riflessologo / la riflessologa**	to relax **rilassarsi**
masseuse **la massaggiatrice**	remedy **il rimedio**	to massage **massaggiare**
chiropractor **il chiropratico / la chiropratica**	reiki **il reiki**	to meditate **meditare**

YOU SHOULD KNOW...

Homeopathy is the most popular alternative therapy in Italy, followed by herbal remedies and acupuncture. It is possible to find a wide range of homeopathic and herbal remedies in Italian pharmacies.

GENERAL

essential oil
l'olio essenziale *m*

herbal medicine
la fitoterapia

homeopathy
l'omeopatia *f*

acupuncture
l'agopuntura *f*

chiropractic
la chiropratica

hypnotherapy
l'ipnoterapia *f*

massage
il massaggio

meditation
la meditazione

osteopathy
l'osteopatia *f*

thalassotherapy
la talassoterapia

reflexology
la riflessologia

traditional Chinese
medicine
**la medicina
tradizionale
cinese**

If you intend to travel to Italy with your pet, they must be microchipped and vaccinated against rabies, and have a pet passport. You cannot take your pet into Italy until 21 days after a rabies vaccination if it is a first vaccination.

YOU MIGHT SAY...

My dog has been hurt.
Il mio cane si è fatto male.

My cat is unwell.
Il gatto sta male.

YOU MIGHT HEAR...

What's the problem?
Può dirmi qual'è il problema?

Is your pet microchipped?
Il suo animale domestico ha un microchip?

YOU SHOULD KNOW...

Dogs and cats can travel on Italian trains in a pet carrier, but only if they weigh less than 6 kg.

VOCABULARY

vet
il veterinario

pet
l'animale domestico *m*

flea
la pulce

tick
la zecca

rabies vaccination
la vaccinazione antirabbica

microchip
il microchip

pet passport
il passaporto per animali domestici

quarantine
la quarantena

to go to the vet
andare dal veterinario

to spay/neuter
sterilizzare

to put to sleep
sopprimere

E-collar
il collare elisabettiano

flea collar
il collare antipulci

pet carrier
il trasportino per animali domestici

Italy's varied, colourful and dramatic landscape makes it a
fantastic place to explore for anyone who loves the great
outdoors, as well as offering a wealth of biodiversity. There are
over 800 long-distance hiking trails the length and breadth of
the country, as well as endless opportunities for day hikes and
shorter walks, offering walkers a chance to discover the Italian
countryside for themselves. Numerous nature reserves and
natural marine parks can be found throughout Italy.

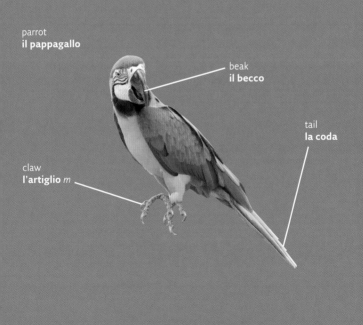

parrot
il pappagallo

beak
il becco

tail
la coda

claw
l'artiglio *m*

YOU MIGHT SAY...

Is there a park/nature reserve nearby?
C'è un parco / una riserva naturale qui vicino?

What is the scenery like?
Com'è il paesaggio?

I enjoy being outdoors.
Mi piace stare all'aria aperta.

YOU MIGHT HEAR...

The scenery is beautiful/rugged.
Il paesaggio è splendido / irregolare.

This is a protected area.
È un'area protetta.

I'd recommend visiting...
Consiglierei di visitare...

VOCABULARY

animal **l'animale** *m*	paw **la zampa**	beak **il becco**
bird **l'uccello** *m*	hoof **lo zoccolo**	cold-blooded **a sangue freddo**
fish **il pesce**	snout **il muso**	warm-blooded **a sangue caldo**
species **la specie**	mane **la criniera**	to bark **abbaiare**
nature reserve **la riserva naturale**	tail **la coda**	to purr **fare le fusa**
scenery **il paesaggio**	claw **l'artiglio** *m*	to growl **ringhiare**
zoo **lo zoo**	horn **il corno**	to roar **ruggire**
fur **la pelliccia**	feather **la piuma**	to chirp **cinguettare**
wool **la lana**	wing **l'ala** *f*	to buzz **ronzare**

DOMESTIC ANIMALS AND BIRDS
ANIMALI DOMESTICI E UCCELLI

Over half of Italian households have at least one pet, with dogs being the most popular. Businesses are generally accepting of people travelling with animals: hotels will often quote a rate for pets and restaurants tend to be dog-friendly. Some public areas, like parks and beaches, may be off-limits for dogs.

YOU MIGHT SAY...

Do you have any pets?
Ha animali domestici?

Is it OK to bring my pet?
Posso portare il mio animale domestico?

This is my guide dog/assistance dog.
Questo è il mio cane guida / di assistenza.

YOU MIGHT HEAR...

I have/don't have a pet.
Ho / Non ho un animale domestico.

I'm allergic to pet hair.
Sono allergico ai peli degli animali domestici.

Animals are not allowed.
Gli animali non sono ammessi.

VOCABULARY

owner
il proprietario / la proprietaria

farmer
l'agricoltore *m*

farm
l'azienda agricola *f*

barn
il granaio

meadow
il prato

hay
il fieno

straw
la paglia

lamb
l'agnello *m*

calf
il vitello

foal
il puledro

kitten
il gattino

puppy
il cucciolo

guide dog
il cane guida

to have a pet
avere un animale domestico

to go to the vet
andare dal veterinario

to walk the dog
portare a spasso il cane

to farm
allevare

budgerigar
il pappagallino ondulato

canary
il canarino

cat
il gatto

dog
il cane

ferret
il furetto

goldfish
il pesciolino rosso

guinea pig
il porcellino d'India

hamster
il criceto

parrot
il pappagallo

pony
il pony

rabbit
il coniglio

rat
il ratto

FARM ANIMALS

bull
il toro

chicken
il pollo

cow
la mucca

donkey
l'asino *m*

duck
l'anatra *f*

goat
la capra

goose
l'oca *f*

horse
il cavallo

pig
il maiale

sheep
la pecora

sheepdog
il cane da pastore

turkey
il tacchino

aquarium
l'**acquario** *m*

cage
la **gabbia**

catflap
la **gattaiola**

collar
il **collare**

dog basket
la **cuccia**

hutch
la **gabbia**

kennel
la **cuccia**

lead
il **guinzaglio**

litter tray
la **lettiera**

muzzle
la **museruola**

pet food
il **cibo per animali domestici**

stable
la **stalla**

alligator
l'alligatore *m*

crocodile
il coccodrillo

frog
la rana

gecko
il geco

iguana
l'iguana *f*

lizard
la lucertola

newt
il tritone

salamander
la salamandra

snake
il serpente

toad
il rospo

tortoise
la tartaruga

turtle
**la tartaruga
acquatica**

badger
il tasso

bat
il pipistrello

boar
il cinghiale

deer
il cervo

fox
la volpe

hare
la lepre

hedgehog
il riccio

mole
la talpa

mouse
il topo

otter
la lontra

squirrel
lo scoiattolo

wolf
il lupo

bear
l'orso *m*

camel
il cammello

chimpanzee
lo scimpanzé

elephant
l'elefante *m*

giraffe
la giraffa

gorilla
il gorilla

hippopotamus
l'ippopotamo *m*

kangaroo
il canguro

lion
il leone

monkey
la scimmia

rhinoceros
il rinoceronte

tiger
la tigre

blackbird
il merlo

crane
la gru

crow
il corvo

dove
la colomba

eagle
l'aquila *f*

finch
il fringuello

flamingo
il fenicottero

gull
il gabbiano

hawk
il falco

heron
l'airone *m*

kingfisher
il martin pescatore

lark
l'allodola *f*

ostrich
lo struzzo

owl
il gufo

peacock
il pavone

pelican
il pellicano

penguin
il pinguino

pigeon
il piccione

puffin
la fratercula

robin
il pettirosso

sparrow
il passero

stork
la cicogna

swan
il cigno

thrush
il tordo

VOCABULARY

swarm **lo sciame**	cobweb **la ragnatela**	to buzz **ronzare**
colony **la colonia**	insect bite **la puntura d'insetto**	to sting **pungere**

ant
la formica

bee
l'ape *f*

beetle
il coleottero

butterfly
la farfalla

caterpillar
il bruco

centipede
il millepiedi

cockroach
lo scarafaggio

cricket
il grillo

dragonfly
la libellula

earthworm
il lombrico

fly
la mosca

grasshopper
la cavalletta

ladybird
la coccinella

mayfly
l'efemera *f*

mosquito
la zanzara

moth
la falena

slug
la lumaca

snail
la chiocciola

spider
il ragno

wasp
la vespa

woodlouse
l'onisco *m*

coral
il corallo

crab
il granchio

dolphin
il delfino

eel
l'anguilla *f*

jellyfish
la medusa

killer whale
l'orca marina *f*

lobster
l'aragosta *f*

seal
la foca

sea urchin
il riccio

shark
lo squalo

starfish
la stella marina

whale
la balena

VOCABULARY

stalk **il gambo**	bud **il bocciolo**	bark **la corteccia**
leaf **la foglia**	wood **il legno**	root **la radice**
petal **il petalo**	branch **il ramo**	seed **il seme**
pollen **il polline**	trunk **il tronco**	bulb **il bulbo**

YOU SHOULD KNOW...

In Italy, you should always give an odd number of flowers, but never chrysanthemums, as they are associated with cemeteries.

FLOWERS

buttercup
il ranuncolo

carnation
il garofano

chrysanthemum
il crisantemo

daffodil
il narciso

daisy
la margherita

hyacinth
il giacinto

lily
il giglio

orchid
l'orchidea *f*

pansy
la viola

poppy
il papavero

primrose
la primula

rose
la rosa

sunflower
il girasole

tulip
il tulipano

violet
la violetta

PLANTS AND TREES

chestnut
il castagno

cypress
il cipresso

fir
l'abete *m*

fungus
il fungo

grapevine
la vite

ivy
l'edera *f*

lavender
la lavanda

lilac
il lillà

moss
il muschio

oak
la quercia

olive
l'ulivo *m*

pine
il pino

plane
il platano

poplar
il pioppo

willow
il salice

233

VOCABULARY

landscape **il paesaggio**	estuary **l'estuario** m	rural **rurale**
earth **la terra**	air **l'aria** f	urban **urbano**
soil **il terreno**	atmosphere **l'atmosfera** f	polar **polare**
mud **il fango**	sunrise **l'alba** f	alpine **alpino**
water **l'acqua** f	sunset **il tramonto**	tropical **tropicale**

LAND

cave
la grotta

desert
il deserto

farmland
il terreno agricolo

forest
la foresta

glacier
il ghiacciaio

grassland
la prateria

hill
la collina

lake
il lago

marsh
la palude

mountain
la montagna

pond
lo stagno

river
il fiume

rocks
le rocce *fpl*

scrub
la boscaglia

stream
il ruscello

valley
la vallata

volcano
il vulcano

waterfall
la cascata

cliff
la scogliera

coast
la costa

coral reef
la barriera corallina

island
l'isola *f*

peninsula
la penisola

rockpool
il ristagno d'acqua tra le rocce

SKY

aurora
l'aurora boreale *f*

clouds
le nuvole

moon
la luna

rainbow
l'arcobaleno *m*

stars
le stelle

sun
il sole

CELEBRATIONS AND FESTIVALS

CELEBRAZIONI E SAGRE

"Facciamo festa!" Everyone loves having a reason to get together and celebrate. In Italy, this usually means great food, the company of family and friends, and a glass or two of wine. In addition to the usual well-known holidays, there is also a wealth of Italian customs and traditions associated with the various holidays and festivals throughout the year.

costume
il costume

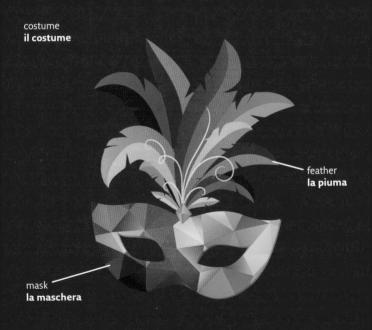

feather
la piuma

mask
la maschera

YOU MIGHT SAY/HEAR...

Congratulations!
Congratulazioni!

Best wishes.
Tanti auguri.

Well done!
Bravo!

Thank you.
Grazie.

Cheers!
Salute!

You're very kind.
È molto gentile.

Happy birthday!
Buon compleanno!

Cheers to you too!
Salute a lei!

Happy anniversary!
Buon anniversario!

VOCABULARY

occasion
l'occasione *f*

religious holiday
la festività religiosa

good/bad news
le buone / cattive notizie

birthday
il compleanno

celebration
la celebrazione

to celebrate
celebrare

birthday party
la festa di compleanno

wedding anniversary
l'anniversario di matrimonio *m*

to throw a party
fare una festa

public holiday
la festa nazionale

surprise party
la festa a sorpresa

to toast
brindare a

YOU SHOULD KNOW...

In Italy, as well as celebrating a person's birthday, family and friends may also celebrate a person's name day ("onomastico") – the feast day for the saint whose name a person shares. This practice has become less common in recent years, especially in the north.

bouquet of flowers
il mazzo di fiori

box of chocolates
la scatola di cioccolatini

bunting
i festoni

cake
la torta

champagne
lo spumante

confetti
i coriandoli

decorations
le decorazioni

fireworks
i fuochi d'artificio

gift
il regalo

greetings card
il bigliettino d'auguri

party
la festa

streamers
le stelle filanti

239

There are 12 official public holidays per year in Italy. While these don't automatically shift if they fall on a weekend, it is commonplace to take an additional Friday or Monday off if the holiday falls on Thursday or Tuesday. This is called "fare il ponte" (literally, "to make the bridge").

YOU MIGHT SAY/HEAR...

Is it a holiday today?
È un giorno festivo oggi?

What are your plans for the holiday?
Quali sono i suoi programmi per le vacanze?

What are you celebrating today?
Cosa si festeggia oggi?

Happy Easter!
Buona Pasqua!

I wish you...
Le auguro...

Happy holidays!
Buone feste!

And to you, too!
Anche a lei!

April Fool!
Pesce d'aprile!

VOCABULARY

birth **la nascita**	wedding anniversary **l'anniversario di matrimonio** *m*	April Fool's Day **il giorno del pesce d'aprile**
baptism **il battesimo**	relocation **il trasferimento**	May Day **il Primo Maggio**
graduation **la laurea**	retirement **andare in pensione**	Valentine's Day **il giorno di San Valentino**
finding a job **trovare un lavoro**	funeral **il funerale**	to have a child **avere un bambino**
engagement **il fidanzamento ufficiale**	Mother's Day **la Festa della Mamma**	to pass your driving test **superare l'esame di guida**
marriage **il matrimonio**	Father's Day **la Festa del Papà**	
wedding **le nozze**	Halloween **il Halloween**	

Liberation Day ("la Festa della Liberazione") is celebrated on April 25th to mark the liberation of Italy from occupation in 1945. Republic Day ("la Festa della Repubblica") is on June 2nd and marks the birth of the Italian Republic in 1946. A very important holiday is "Ferragosto", August 15th, which is the Feast of the Assumption. Many Italians take their summer holidays around this time.

All Saints' Day
il giorno di Ognissanti

Diwali
il Diwali

Easter
la Pasqua

Eid al-Fitr
l'Eid al-Fitr *m*

Hanukkah
l'Hanukkah *f*

Holi
l'Holi *m*

Mardi Gras
il martedì grasso

Passover
la Pasqua ebraica

Ramadan
il Ramadan

Christmas is celebrated on December 25th in Italy. Many families will also gather to have dinner on Christmas Eve after attending a late mass, especially in the south. Christmas cards are not commonly sent in Italy and the festival is generally more low-key than in English-speaking countries.

YOU MIGHT SAY/HEAR...

Merry Christmas!
Buon Natale!

Happy New Year!
Buon anno!

VOCABULARY

Christmas Eve **la vigilia di Natale**	Christmas card **il biglietto di Natale**	New Year's Day **il Capodanno**
Christmas Day **il giorno di Natale**	New Year's Eve **la vigilia di Capodanno**	New Year's card **il biglietto di auguri per Capodanno**

YOU SHOULD KNOW...

The feast of the Epiphany ("Epifania") on January 6th is a public holiday in Italy and is at least as important as Christmas for many Italians. Traditionally, on the night before Epiphany, an old woman called "La Befana" delivers gifts to good children (bad children would get a lump of coal, these days generally replaced by sweets resembling coal).

bauble
la pallina natalizia

Befana
la Befana

Christmas dinner
il cenone di Natale

Christmas lights
le luci di Natale

Christmas tree
l'albero di Natale *m*

Epiphany
l'Epifania *f*

Father Christmas/
Santa Claus
Babbo Natale

mistletoe
il vischio

Nativity scene
il presepio

tinsel
l'orpello *m*

wreath
la ghirlanda

Yule log
**il tronchetto di
Natale**

Carnivals are held across Italy to celebrate "martedì grasso" (Shrove Tuesday), just ahead of Lent. The most high-profile of these is in Venice, but in many places children dress up in fancy dress and play tricks, hence the expression "a Carnevale ogni scherzo vale" (anything goes at carnival time).

carnival doughnuts
le castagnole

carnival float
il carro di Carnevale

costume
il costume

face paint
la pittura facciale

funfair
il luna park

headdress
il copricapo

mask
la maschera

parade
la sfilata

street performer
l'artista di strada *m*

A&E 206
abdomen 196
ABOUT YOU 9
accessible parking
    space 24
accessories 103
accordion 158
acoustic guitar 158
acupuncture 215
aerial 50
aeroplane 40
airbag 29
air bed 153
airport 40
AIR TRAVEL 39
alligator 223
All Saints' Day 241
almond biscuits 88
ALTERNATIVE
    THERAPIES 214
aluminium foil 54
amaretti biscuits 88
ambulance 206
American football
    189
AMPHIBIANS AND
    REPTILES 223
anchor 43
anchovy 83
ankle 195
ant 228
antifreeze 29
antiperspirant 95
antique shop 111
antiseptic 210
antiseptic cream 94
apartment block 47
apple 78
apple cake 120
apricot 78
aquarium 222
archery 189
arm 196
armbands 179
armchair 53, 61
art gallery 145
artichoke 81
ARTS AND CRAFTS 164
asparagus 81
assistant referee 173
assorted cold meats
    and cheeses 118
athlete 186
ATHLETICS 186
ATM 136
aubergine 81

aurora 236
baby bath 99
baby blanket 213
baby food 98
BABY GOODS 97
babygro® 97, 213
baby lotion 98
baby's bottle 98
baby seat 99
baby walker 99
back 197
backgammon 163
badger 224
badminton 176
badminton racket
    176
baggage reclaim 40
BAKERY AND
    PATISSERIE 88
baking tray 55
balcony 45
ball boy 177
ballet 147
ball girl 177
ball of wool 166
banana 69, 78
bandage 94, 191, 210
BANK 135
banknotes 72, 136
bar 122, 147
barbecue 153
barber's 111
baseball cap 107
baseball game 189
BASICS 8, 18, 46, 70,
    114, 142, 168, 192,
    218, 238
basket 69, 74, 175
BASKETBALL 175
basketball 175
basketball court 175
basketball game 175
basketball player 175
basketball shoes 175
bass drum 158
bass guitar 158
bat 224
bath 63
bath mat 62
BATHROOM 62
bathroom 63
bath towel 62
bauble 242
BEACH 154
beach ball 155
beach hut 155

beach towel 155
beak 217
bear 225
beauty salon 111
bed 61
BEDROOM 60
bedroom 61
bedside lamp 61
bedside table 61
bee 228
beefburger 87
beer 76
beetle 228
Befana 242
bell 33
belt 107
bib 97
BICYCLE 32
bicycle 33
bidet 63
big toe 195
bike lock 33
bikini 105, 155
bill 122
bin bag 54
birdbox 66
BIRDS 226
biscuits 74
black 7
blackberry 79
blackbird 226
blade 17
blanket 60
blister 209
block of flats 45
blood pressure
    monitor 201
blouse 105
blue 7
blueberry 79
Bluetooth® speaker
    158
Blu-ray® player 52
blusher 96
boar 225
board game 163
boarding card 41
BODY 194
body 196, 197
bodyboarding 179
boiler 49
bonnet 29
book 100
bookcase 52
bookshop 111
boot 22

bootees 97
boots 34, 108
bouquet of flowers
    239
boutique 111
bowl 59
bowling 163
bowls 189
box 138
boxer shorts 105
boxing gloves 184
boxing ring 184
boxing shoes 184
box of chocolates
    239
bra 105
bracelet 107
braces 203
brake 33
bread 69
bread basket 122
bread bin 54
bread rolls 88, 116
BREAKFAST 115
breastbone 199
bridge 24
broad beans 81
broccoli 81
bruise 209
brush 67
bucket 67
bucket and spade
    155
budgerigar 220
bull 221
bumper 22
bungalow 47
bunk beds 60
bunting 239
buoy 43
bureau de change
    136
burger 126
burn 209
burrata 90
BUS 30
bus 31
bus shelter 31
BUTCHER'S 86
butter 92, 116
buttercup 231
butterfly 228
butter knife 124
buttocks 197
buttons 166
cabbage 81

cabin 41
cabinet 63
caciocavallo 90
caciotta 90
café 139
cafeteria 131
cafetière 55
cage 222
cake 89, 239
calculator 133
calf 197
camel 225
camera 145
camera lens 161
CAMPING 152
camping stove 153
campus 131
canal boat 44
canary 220
canoe 44
canoeing 179
canvas 165
cappuccino 115
capsule 94
CAR 20
car 22
caravan 153
cardigan 105
card reader 72
cards 163
carnation 231
CARNIVAL 244
carnival 147
carnival doughnuts
    244
carnival float 244
car park 24
carriage 37
carrot 81
car showroom 111
CAR TROUBLE 27
car wash 25
casino 147
casserole dish 55
castle 145
cat 220
caterpillar 228
catflap 222
cathedral 139, 145
cauliflower 81
cave 234
ceiling fan 49
celery 81
cello 158
centipede 228
centre circle 167

cereal 116
chain 33
chair 122
champagne 239
champagne flute 59
changing bag 98
changing room 171
charger 128
check-in desk 41
cheek 195
cheese knife 122
CHEESE SHOP 90
cherry 79
chess 163
chest 196
chestnut tree 232
chicken 221
chicken breast 87
chilli 81
chimney 50
chimpanzee 225
chin 195
chips 119
chiropractic 215
chisel 109
chocolate 76
chocolate mousse 120
chocolate spread 116
choir 160
chop 87
chopping board 55
CHRISTMAS AND NEW YEAR 243
Christmas dinner 242
Christmas lights 243
Christmas tree 243
chrysanthemum 231
church 139
ciabatta 89
cigar 100
cigarette 100
cinema 147
city map 145
clam 85
clarinet 158
claw 217
cliff 236
climbing 189
clingfilm 54
clock radio 60
cloth 67
clothes horse 67
clothes pegs 67
CLOTHING AND FOOTWEAR 104
clouds 236
coach 31
coast 236
coat 105

coat hanger 60
cockpit 17, 41
cockroach 228
cod 83
coffee 115
coffee pot 55
coffee table 53
coffee with milk 113
coins 72
colander 55
collage 164
collar 222
collarbone 199
colouring pencils 130
comb 96
COMBAT SPORTS 184
comedy show 147
comic book 100
COMMUNICATION AND IT 127
compact camera 161
computer 128
concert 148
conditioner 95
condom 94
conductor 160
confectionery 100
conference centre 139
confetti 239
contact lens case 205
contact lenses 205
cooking 143
cool box 153
coral 230
coral reef 236
corkscrew 55
corridor 150
cosmetics 103
costume 237, 244
cot 99
cotton bud 98
cotton wool 98
couchette 37
cough mixture 94
counters 163
courgette 81
courthouse 139
couscous 74
cow 221
crab 85, 230
crampons 182
crane 226
crash helmet 34
crayfish 85
cream 92
cream soup 118
credit card 136
cricket 189, 228
crispbread 116
crisps 76

crochet hook 166
crocodile 223
croissant 89, 116
crossbar 33
cross trainer 171
crossword 163
crow 226
crutches 206
cucumber 81
cup 113
cup and saucer 59
cupboard 57
(cured) sausage 87
curtains 52, 61
cushion 53
custard tart with pine nuts 120
custard-filled croissant 89
cut 209
cymbals 159
cypress 232
daffodil 231
daisy 231
darts 163
dashboard 23
DAYS, MONTHS, AND SEASONS 15
debit card 72
deckchair 155
decking 64
decorations 239
deep-fried rice balls 118
deer 224
deli 111
dental floss 203
dental nurse 203
dentist 203
dentist's chair 203
dentist's drill 203
DENTIST'S SURGERY 202
dentures 203
DEPARTMENT STORE 102
departure board 37, 41
desert 234
desk 133
desk lamp 133
dessert fork 124
dessert spoon 124
dice 163
DINING ROOM 58
dinner plate 124
discus 186
dishwasher 57
display cabinet 52
diving board 179
Diwali 241

DIY 143
DIY STORE 109
"do not disturb" sign 150
doctor 193
DOCTOR'S SURGERY 200
dog 220
dog basket 222
dolphin 230
DOMESTIC ANIMALS AND BIRDS 219
dominoes 163
donkey 221
door 22
doorbell 51
double bass 159
double room 150
doughnut 89
dove 226
dragonfly 228
draining board 57
drainpipe 50
draughts 163
drawer 57
dress 106
dressing 210
dressing gown 106
dressing table 60
drip 207
driveway 50
DRIVING 24
drone 161
drops 94
DSLR camera 161
duck 221
dumbbells 171
dummy 99
dustbin 68
dustpan 68
duty-free shop 41
duvet 61
DVD player 52
eagle 226
ear 195
earphones 158
earrings 108
earthworm 229
easel 165
Easter 241
EATING OUT 121
éclair 89
E-collar 216
EDUCATION 129
eel 230
egg 92
Eid al-Fitr 241
elbow 197
electric drill 109
electric guitar 159
electronics store 111
elephant 225

embroidery 164
emergency phone 29
Emmenthal 90
ENTRANCE 51
envelope 100
envelope 138
Epiphany 243
eraser 130
espresso 115
essential oil 214
estate agency 111
EVENINGS OUT 146
examination room 201
examination table 201
exchange rate 136
exercise bike 171
exercise book 130
extension cable 49
eye 195
eye chart 205
eye drops 205
eyeliner 96
eyeshadow 96
eye test 205
fabric 166
fabric scissors 166
face 195, 196
face cloth 62
face paint 244
FAMILY AND FRIENDS 10
farmhouse 47
farmland 234
fashion 103
FAST FOOD 125
Father Christmas 243
feather 237
femur 199
fence 66
fencing 185
ferret 220
ferry 44
FERRY AND BOAT TRAVEL 42
fibula 199
fig 79
filing cabinet 133
finch 226
finger 195
fingernail 195
fir 232
fireplace 53
fire station 139
fireworks 239
first-aid kit 191, 193
fishing 189
fish knife 122
FISHMONGER'S 83
fish soup 118

fizzy drink 76
flamingo 226
flea collar 216
flip-flops 155
flippers 156, 179
florist's 111
flowerpot 66
flowers 66
FLOWERS, PLANTS,
    AND TREES 231
flute 159
fly 229
flysheet 141
focaccia 89
folder 133
fold-up chair 153
fontina 90
food and drink 103
food processor 55
foot 195, 196
FOOTBALL 172
football 173
football boots 173
football match 172
football pitch 167,
    173
football player 173
footstool 53
footwear 103
forehead 195
forest 234
fork 124
formula milk 98
foundation 96
fountain 140
fox 224
fracture 209
frame 33
frames 205
FRESH AND DAIRY
    PRODUCTS 73
fridge-freezer 57
fried courgette
    flowers 118
fries 126
frog 223
front door 50
front light 33
FRUIT AND
    VEGETABLES 78
fruit juice 76
fruit salad 116
fruit tart 120
frying pan 55
fuel gauge 23
fuel pump 25
funfair 148, 244
fungus 233
furniture 103
furniture store 111
fusebox 49
gable 50

GAMES 162
gaming 143
gangway 43
garage 29, 50
GARDEN 64
garden 66
garden centre 111
garden fork 64
garden furniture 66
garden hose 64
gardening 143
gardening gloves 64
gardens 145
garden shed 64
garlic 82
gate 50, 66
gears 33
gearstick 23
gecko 223
GENERAL HEALTH
    AND WELLBEING 11
gift 239
giraffe 225
glacier 234
glasses 205
glasses case 205
glove compartment
    23
gloves 108
goal 167, 173
goalkeeper 173
goalkeeper's gloves
    173
goat 221
goat's cheese 90
goggles 179
goldfish 220
GOLF 188
golf bag 188
golf ball 188
golf buggy 188
golf club 188
goose 221
gorgonzola 91
gorilla 225
GP 201
grape 79
grapefruit 79
grapevine 233
grasshopper 229
grassland 234
grater 55
gravy boat 58
graze 209
green 7
green beans 82
greenhouse 64
green salad 119
greetings card
    101, 239
grilled sea bream 119
groundsheet 141

guard 37
guidebook 145
guinea pig 220
gull 226
gums 203
gutter 50
guy rope 141
gym ball 171
gymnastics 189
hair 195
hairbrush 96
hairdresser's 112
hairdryer 60
hairspray 96
ham 87
hammer 109
hamster 220
hand 195, 196
handbag 108
handball 189
handbrake 23
handle 113
handlebars 33
hand mixer 55
hand towel 62
Hanukkah 241
harbour 43
hare 224
harp 159
hawk 226
head 196
headdress 244
headguard 184
headlight 22
headphones 158
headrest 23
health food shop 112
heater 49
hedgehog 224
heel 195
helicopter 17
helmet 33
helmet cam 34
herbal medicine 214
herb chopper 55
herbs 74
heron 226
herring 83
highchair 99
HIGH DAYS AND
    HOLIDAYS 240
high heels 108
high jump 186
hill 235
hip 197
hippopotamus 225
hi-viz vest 29
hob 57
hockey 189
hoe 65
hog roast 87
holdall 41

hole punch 133
Holi 241
homeopathy 214
honey 74
horse 221
horse racing 189
HOPSITAL 206
hospital 140, 193
hospital bed 207
hospital trolley 207
hot chocolate 115
hot dog 126
HOTEL 149
hotel 140
HOUSE 48
house 50
HOUSEWORK 67
humerus 199
hurdles 186
hutch 222
hyacinth 231
hypnotherapy 215
ice axe 182
ice cream 120
ice hockey 189
ice pack 210
ice skates 182
ice skating 182
icing sugar 74
ignition 23
iguana 223
ILLNESS 211
incubator 213
indicator 22
inflatable dinghy 44
INJURY 208
ink 165
in/out tray 133
insect repellent 94
instant coffee 74
intercom 51
IN TOWN 139
iron 68
ironing board 68
island 236
ivy 233
jack 29
jacket 106
jam 74, 116
javelin 186
jaw 195
jeans 106
jellyfish 230
jet ski 179
jetty 43
jeweller's 112
jewellery-making 164
jigsaw puzzle 163
jogging 143
jogging bottoms 106
joint 87
judo 185

jug of water 123
jumper 106
jump leads 29
junction 25
kangaroo 225
karate 185
kayak 44
kayaking 180
kennel 222
kerb 25
ketchup 74
kettle bell 171
keyboard 159
key card 151
kickboxing 185
killer whale 230
kingfisher 226
KITCHEN 54
kitchen 57
kitchen roll 54
kitchenware 103
kiwi fruit 79
knee 196
kneecap 199
knife 124
knife and fork 59
knitting needles 166
knuckle 195
labour suite 213
lace-up shoes 108
ladle 56
ladybird 229
lake 235
LAND, SEA, AND SKY
    234
lane 25
laptop 133
lark 226
lasagne 118
lattice-top pie 89
laundrette 140
laundry basket 61
lavender 233
lawn 66
lawnmower 65
lead 222
leather gloves 34
leather goods 103
leather jacket 34
lecture hall 131
lecturer 131
leek 82
leg 196
leggings 106
leisure centre 169
lemon 79
lemon sole 84
letter 138
letterbox 51
level crossing 25
library 131, 140
lifebuoy 43

lifeguard 179
lifejacket 44, 180
light bulb 49
lighting 103
light railway 37
lilac 233
lily 232
line judge 177
liner 44
lingerie 103
lion 225
lip balm 96
lipstick 96
listening to music 143
litter tray 222
lizard 223
lobster 85, 230
locker 171
locomotive 37
long jump 186
LOUNGE 52
lounge 53
lozenge 94
luggage rack 37
luggage trolley 41
mackerel 84
magazine 101
MAIN MEALS 117
MAMMALS 224
mango 79
map 19, 101
Mardi Gras 241
margarine 92
marina 44
MARINE CREATURES 230
MARKET 77
marmalade 74
marsh 235
mascara 96
mascarpone 91
masher 56
mask 237, 244
massage 215
matches 153
mattress 61
mayfly 229
mayonnaise 75
measuring jug 56
meatballs in tomato sauce 119
meat roulade 119
mechanic 29
medal 169
medicine 94, 193
meditation 215
melon 79
menu 123
meter 50
metro 37
microwave 57

midwife 213
milk 92
mince 87
minibar 151
MINIBEASTS 228
minibus 31
mirror 61, 63
mistletoe 243
mittens 97
mixed salad 120
mixed seafood 118
mixing bowl 56
mobile 99
model-making 164
mole 224
monitor 207
monkey 225
monument 145
moon 236
mooring 44
mop 68
mortadella 87
Moses basket 99
mosque 140
mosquito 229
moss 233
moth 229
MOTORBIKE 34
motorbike 34
motorcycle racing 190
motorhome 153
motor racing 190
motorway 25
mountain 235
mouse 224
mouth 195
mouthguard 184
mouth organ 159
mouthwash 95, 203
mozzarella 91
muesli 116
museum 145
mushroom 82
MUSIC 157
musical 148
musician 160
mussel 85
muzzle 222
nails 109
nail varnish 96
napkin 58, 124
nappy 98, 213
nappy cream 98
Nativity scene 243
neck 196
neck brace 210
necklace 108
nectarine 79
needle and thread 166
netball 190

NEWSAGENT 100
newspaper 101
newt 223
nightclub 148
noodles 75
nose 17, 195
notebook 101
notepad 133
number plate 22
nurse 193
nuts 76
nuts and bolts 109
oak 233
oars 180
octopus 85
OFFICE 132
office block 140
official 169
oil paint 165
ointment 210
olive 233
olive oil 75
olives 76
omelette 126
onion 82
opera 148
operating theatre 207
optician 205
OPTICIAN'S 204
optician's 112
orange 79
orange juice 115
orchestra 160
orchid 232
ornament 53
osteopathy 215
ostrich 227
OTHER SHOPS 111
OTHER SPORTS 189
otter 224
oven 57
owl 227
oxygen mask 207
oyster 85
package 138
padded envelope 138
paddle 180
paddleboarding 180
paint 109
paintbrush 110, 165
paint roller 110
palette 165
palm 195
pancakes 126
pancetta 87
panettone 89
panino 126
pannacotta 120
pansy 232
pants 106
paper 130, 165

paper bag 72
paper clip 134
parade 244
paramedic 193
parasol 65, 155
parfait 120
park 140
parking meter 25
parking space 25
Parmesan 91
parrot 27, 220
party 239
passion fruit 80
Passover 241
passport 41
pasta 75, 118
pasta machine 56
pastels 165
patient 193
path 66
patio 66
pavement 25
peach 80
peacock 227
pear 80
peas 82
pecorino 91
pedal 33
pedal bin 54
peeler 56
pelican 227
pelvis 199
pen 101, 130, 165
penalty box 167
pencil 101, 130, 165
pencil case 131
penguin 227
peninsula 236
pepper 75
pepper mill 58
pet carrier 216
pet food 222
petrol station 25
pet shop 112
pharmacist 193
PHARMACY 193
pharmacy 193
phone shop 112
photocopier 134
PHOTOGRAPHY 161
piano 159
picnic blanket 153
picture 53
pig 221
pigeon 227
pill 94
pillow 61
pilot 41
pine 233
pineapple 80
pins 166
piste 183

pizza 126
plane 233
plant pot 65
plaster 94, 191, 210
plaster cast 207
plastic bag 72
plate 59
platform 37
playground 140
pliers 110
plum 80
podium 169
pole vault 187
police station 140
pond 235
pony 220
popcorn 76
poplar 233
poppy 232
pork cutlet 119
porter 37, 151
postal worker 138
postbox 138
postcard 101, 138
POST OFFICE 137
potato 82
pothole 25
pottery 164
powder 96
practice nurse 201
pram 99
prawn 85
PREGNANCY 212
pregnancy test 213
primrose 232
printer 134
profiteroles 120
promenade 156
provolone 91
pruners 65
puffin 227
pump 33
punchbag 184
pushchair 99
putter 188
puzzle book 101
pyjamas 106
quilt 61
rabbit 220
RACKET SPORTS 176
radiator 50
radicchio 82
radio 52
radius 199
RAIL TRAVEL 35
rainbow 236
Ramadan 241
raspberry 79
rat 220
razor 95
reading 143
rearview mirror 23

receipt 72
reception 151
receptionist 151
record shop 112
red 7
red card 173
redcurrant 80
red pepper 82
red wine glass 124
referee 169
reflector 33
reflexology 215
refreshments
    trolley 72
relay 187
remote control 52
restaurant 148
restaurant car 37
reusable shopping
    bag 72
rhinoceros 225
ribs 199
rice 75
ricotta 91
ring binder 134
risotto 118
river 235
road 26
roast chicken 119
roast potatoes 120
robin 227
rockpool 236
rocks 235
rolling pin 56
roof 22, 45, 50
rope 182
rose 232
rotor 17
roundabout 26
rowing boat 44
rowing machine 171
rubber gloves 68
rug 53, 61
RUGBY 174
rugby 174
rugby ball 174
rugby field 174
rugby goalposts 174
rugby player 174
ruler 131
running track 187
runway 41
rusk 98
saddle 33
safe 151
safety deposit box
    136
safety pin 166
sailing boat 44
salad bowl 58
salamander 223
salmon 84

salopettes 183
salt 75
salt and pepper 123
salt cellar 58
salt cod 84
sand 155
sandals 108
sandcastle 156
sanitary towel 95
Santa Claus 243
sardine 84
sat nav 23
saucepan 56
saucer 113
sausage 87
saw 110
saxophone 159
scales 74
scallop 85
scamorza 91
scanner 134
scarf 108
schoolbag 131
scissors 134
scoreboard 169
scourer 68
scratch card 101
screwdriver 110
screws 110
scrub 235
scrum 174
scuba diving 180
SD card 161
sea 155
sea bass 84
sea bream 84
seal 230
seashells 156
seaside 155
seatbelt 23
sea urchin 85, 230
seaweed 156
security alarm 50
semi-detached
    house 47
serving dish 58
sewing basket 166
sewing machine 166
shampoo 95
shark 230
sharpener 131
shaving foam 95
sheep 221
sheepdog 221
sheet music 160
sheets 61
shelves 53
shin 196
shin pads 173
shirt 106
shoe shop 112
shooting 190

shopping 143
shopping mall 112
shorts 106
shot put 187
shoulder 197
shower 63
shower gel 95
shower puff 62
showers 171
shower screen 63
showjumping 190
shrimp 85
shrub 66
shutter 50
shuttlecock 176
sideboard 53
side plate 124
sieve 56
SIGHTSEEING 144
sightseeing bus 145
signal box 37
SIM card 128
singer 160
single room 151
sink 57
skateboarding 190
SKELETON 198
skeleton 199
sketchpad 165
ski boots 183
ski gloves 183
ski goggles 183
ski helmet 183
ski jacket 183
ski poles 183
skipping rope 171
skirt 106
skis 183
ski suit 183
skull 199
sledge 182
sleeping bag 153
sleepsuit 97
sliced beef 119
sliced veal in tuna
    sauce 119
sliding doors 38
sling 210
slippers 108
slug 229
smartphone 128
smoke alarm 50
smoked salmon 118
snail 229
snake 223
snare drum 159
snooker 190
snorkel 156
snorkelling 180
snowboard 183
snowboarding boots
    183

snow chains 29
snowsuit 97
soap 62, 95
socks 107
sofa 53
soft furnishings 103
sole 195
sonographer 213
soundbar 158
soup 118
soup bowl 124
soup spoon 124
spade 65
spanner 110
spare wheel 29
sparkling water 76
sparrow 227
speakers 158
spectators 169
speed camera 26
speedometer 23
spices 75
spider 229
spikes 187
spinach 82
spinach with lemon
    and olive oil 120
spine 199
spirit level 110
spirits 76
splinter 209
sponge 63
spoon 59
sports 143
sportsperson 169
spotlight 57
squash 82, 176
squash ball 176
squash racket 176
squid 85
squirrel 224
stable 222
stadium 169
stamp 101, 138
stands 169
stapler 134
starfish 230
stars 236
starting blocks 187
steak 87, 119
steak knife 123
steering wheel 23
stepladder 110
stethoscope 201
sticky notes 134
sticky tape 134
still water 76
sting 209
stir-fried chicory 120
stitches 207
stopwatch 187

stork 227
strawberry 80
stream 235
streamers 239
street performer 244
student 131
studio flat 47
sugar 75
suitcase 41
sun 236
sunbed 155
sunburn 209
sunflower 232
sunglasses 156
sunhat 156
suntan lotion 94, 156
SUPERMARKET 73
surfboard 180
surfing 180
sushi 126
swan 227
sweatshirt 107
sweets 76
swimming cap 179
swimming pool 179
swimming trunks
    156, 179
swimsuit 107, 156,
    179
swivel chair 134
synagogue 140
syringe 191, 201
table 123
tablecloth 123
table setting 124
tablet 94, 128, 191
table tennis 190
taekwondo 185
tai chi 185
tail 17, 217
talcum powder 98
taleggio 91
tampon 95
tap 57, 63
tape measure 166
tea 115
teabags 75
team 169
teaspoon 59
tea towel 68
tee 188
teeth 203
teething ring 99
telephone 134
tennis 177
tennis ball 177
tennis court 177
tennis player 177
tennis racket 177
tent 141, 153
tent peg 141
textbook 131

thalassotherapy 215
theatre 148
thermometer 201
thermostat 50
thigh 196
(three-piece) suit 107
thrush 227
thumb 195
tibia 199
ticket 19
ticket barrier 38
ticket machine 38
ticket office 38
tie 107
tiger 225
tights 107
tiles 57, 110
till point 72
TIME 14
timetable 19
tin opener 56
tinsel 243
tiramisu 120
toad 223
toasted sandwich
    126
toaster 56
tobacco 101
toe 195
toenail 195
toilet 63
toilet brush 63
toiletries 151
toilet roll 63
toll point 26
tomato 82
toothbrush 95, 203
toothpaste 95, 203
toothpicks 123

torch 153
tortellini 118
tortoise 223
tour guide 145
tourist office 145
towel rail 63
town hall 140
tow truck 29
toys 103
toyshop 112
track 38
track cycling 190
traditional Chinese
    medicine 215
traffic cone 26
traffic lights 26
traffic warden 26
train 38
trainers 108
train station 38
tram 31
travel agency 112
travel cot 99
travelling 143
treadmill 171
trellis 66
tripod 161
trolley 74
trolley bus 31
trombone 159
trophy 169
trousers 107
trout 84
trowel 65
trumpet 159
T-shirt 107
tuba 160
tulip 232
tumble drier 68

tumbler 59
tuna 84
tunnel 26
turkey 221
turntable 158
turtle 223
TV 53
TV stand 53
tweezers 210
twin room 151
tyre 22, 33
ulna 199
ultrasound 213
umbrella 7
umpire 177
umpire's chair 177
USB stick 134
vacuum cleaner 68
validation machine
    38
valley 235
veal wrapped in
    Parma ham and
    sage 119
vegetable oil 69, 75
Venetian blind 53
vertebrae 199
vest 97
VET 216
vinegar 75
vinegar and oil 123
violet 232
violin 160
volcano 235
volleyball 190
waiter 123
waiting room 201
waitress 123
walking 143

wall light 53
wallpaper 110
ward 207
wardrobe 61
warning triangle 29
wash-hand basin 63
washing line 68
washing machine 68
wasp 229
watching TV/films
    143
watercolours 165
waterfall 235
watering can 65
water glass 124
watermelon 80
water polo 190
waterproof jacket 107
waterskiing 180
WATER SPORTS 178
waves 155
WEATHER 16
weedkiller 65
weightlifting 190
weightlifting bench
    171
WELLBEING 170
Wellington boots 65
wetsuit 180
wet wipes 98
whale 230
wheel 22, 33
wheelbarrow 65
wheelchair 207
whisk 57
whistle 173
white 7
whiteboard 131
white wine glass 124

willow 233
windbreak 156
window 22, 45, 50
windowbox 65
windscreen 22
windscreen wiper 22
windsurfing 180
wine 76
wine glass 59
wine shop 112
wing 22
wing mirror 22
WINTER SPORTS 181
wireless router 128
wok 57
wolf 224
wood-burning stove
    50
wooden spoon 57
woodlouse 229
woodwork 164
woolly hat 108
WORK 12
worktop 57
wreath 243
wrench 110
wrestling 185
wrist 195
X-ray 207
xylophone 160
yacht 44
yellow 7
yellow card 173
yoghurt 92
Yule log 243
zebra crossing 26
Zimmer frame® 207

ITALIAN

abat-jour 61
abete 232
abito 106
abito (a tre pezzi) 107
accensione 23
accessori 103
acciuga 83
aceto 75
aceto e l'olio 123
acqua gassata 76
acqua liscia 76
acquario 222
acquerelli 165
addome 196
aeroplano 40
aeroporto 40
affettati e formaggi
    misti 118

agenzia immobiliare
    111
agenzia viaggi 112
aglio 82
ago e il filo 166
agopuntura 215
airbag 29
airone 226
ala 22
ALBERGHI 149
albergo 140
albero di Natale 243
albicocca 78
album per schizzi 165
alga marina 156
allarme di sicurezza
    50
alligatore 223

allodola 226
alluce 195
altoparlante
    Bluetooth® 158
altoparlanti 158
altri negozi 111
ALTRI SPORT 189
amaretti 88
ambulanza 206
ambulatorio 201
ananas 80
anatra 221
anca 197
ancora 43
andare in canoa 179
andare in kayak 180
anello da dentizione
    99

ANFIBI E RETTILI 223
anguilla 230
anguria 80
ANIMALI DOMESTICI E
    UCCELLI 219
ANIMALI MARINI 230
annaffiatoio 65
ansa 113
antenna 50
antigelo 29
antiquariato 111
antisettico 210
antitraspirante 95
ape 228
apparecchio 203
apriscatole 56
aquila 226
aragosta 85, 230

arancia 79
arancini 118
arbitro 169, 177
arcobaleno 236
area di rigore 167
aringa 83
armadietto 63, 171
armadio 61
armadio espositivo
    52
armonica a bocca
    159
arpa 159
arrampicata 189
arredamento da
    giardino 66
ARTI E MESTIERI 164
articoli da toilette 151

articolo in pelle 103
artiglio 217
artista di strada 244
asciugacapelli 60
asciugamano da bagno 62
asciugamano da mare 155
asciugamano per il viso 62
asciugamano per le mani 62
asciugatrice 68
ascoltare la musica 143
asino 221
asparago 81
aspirapolvere 68
assistente dentale 203
assorbente 95
assorbente interno 95
astuccio 131
atleta 186
ATLETICA 186
aula 131
auricolari 158
aurora boreale 236
ausiliare del traffico 26
AUTOBUS 30
autobus 31
autobus turistico 145
autofficina 29
autolavaggio 25
autosalone 111
autostrada 25
autovelox 26
azzurro 7
Babbo Natale 243
baccalà 84
bacino 199
badminton 176
bagnina 179
bagnino 179
BAGNO 62
bagno 63
bagnoschiuma 95
balcone 45
balena 230
balsamo 95
banana 69, 78
BANCA 135
bancone 122
banconote 72, 136
bar 139
barbiere 111
barca a remi 44
barca a vela 44
barriera corallina 236
baseball 189

basso 158
bastoncini da sci 183
bastone da golf 188
bavaglino 97
becco 217
Befana 242
benda 191, 210
BENESSERE 11, 170
benzinaio 25
berretto con visiera 107
bevanda carbonata 76
biancheria intima 103
bianco 7
biberon 98
biblioteca 131, 140
bicchiere 59
bicchiere per l'acqua 124
bicchiere da vino bianco 124
bicchiere da vino rosso 124
BICICLETTA 32
bicicletta 33
bidè 63
bidone della spazzatura 68
biglietteria 38
biglietteria automatica 38
bigliettino di auguri 101, 239
biglietto 19
bignè 89
bikini 105, 155
bilancia 74
binario 37, 38
birra 76
biscotti 74
biscotti di mandorle 88
biscotto 98
bistecca 87, 119
bivio 25
blocchi di partenza 187
boa 43
bocca 195
boccaglio 156
bocce 189
bodyboard 179
bomba 89
borotalco 98
borsa 108
borsa da golf 188
borsa da viaggio 41
borsa del ghiaccio 210
borsa per il cambio 98

boscaglia 235
bottoni 166
boutique 111
bowling 163
boxer 105
bracciale 107
braccio 196
braccioli 179
broccolo 81
bruciatura 209
bruco 228
buca 25
buca delle lettere 138
bungalow 47
burrata 90
burro 92, 116
burro cacao 96
busta 100, 138
busta di carta 72
busta di plastica 72
busta imbottita 138
busta riciclabile 72
bustine di tè 75
cabina 41
cabina da spiaggia 155
cabina di manovra 38
cabina di pilotaggio 17, 41
cacciavite 110
caciocavallo 90
caciotta 90
caffè 115
caffè e latte 113
caffè solubile 74
caffettiera 131
caffettiera 55
calamaro 85
calciatore 173
CALCIO 172
calcolatrice 133
caldaia 49
calice da vino 59
calzature 103
calzini 107
calzoncini 106
cambio 23
camera doppia 150
camera doppia con letti singoli 151
camera singola 151
cameriera 123
cameriere 123
camicetta 106
camicia 106
camino 53
cammello 225
camminare 143
campanello 33, 51
camper 153

CAMPING 152
campo da calcio 167, 173
campo da pallacanestro 175
campo da tennis 177
campo di rugby 173
campus 131
canarino 220
cancello 50, 64
cane 220
cane da pastore 221
canestro 175
canguro 225
canoa 44
canottiera 97
canotto 44
cantante 160
capanno da giardino 64
capasanta 85
capelli 195
cappello da sole 156
cappello di lana 108
cappotto 105
cappuccino 115
capra 221
capsula 94
caraffa d'acqua 123
caramelle 76
caravan 153
carciofo 81
cardigan 105
caricabatterie 128
carne tritata 87
carota 81
carpenteria 164
carrello 37, 74
carrello ospedaliero 207
carrello portabagagli 41
carriola 65
carro attrezzi 29
carro di Carnevale 244
carrozza 37
carrozzina 99
carta 130, 165
carta di cucina 54
carta di parati 110
carta di credito 72, 136
carta di debito 72, 136
carta d'imbarco 41
carte 163
cartella 133
cartellino giallo 173

cartellino "non disturbare" 150
cartellino rosso 173
cartolina 101, 138
CASA 48
casa 50
casa bifamiliare 47
cascata 235
casco 33
casco da sci 183
casco protettivo 34
caserma dei vigili del fuoco 139
casetta per gli uccelli 66
casinò 147
cassa 72
cassaforte 151
casseruola 55
cassetta delle lettere 51
cassetta di sicurezza 136
cassettiera 61
cassetto 57
castagno 232
castagnole 244
castello 145
castello di sabbia 156
catarifrangente 33
catena 33
catene da neve 29
cattedrale 139, 145
cavalletta 229
cavalletto 165
cavallo 221
cavatappi 55
cavi di avviamento 29
caviglia 195
cavolfiore 81
cavolo 81
cenone di Natale 242
centro commerciale 112
centro conferenze 139
centro sportivo 169
ceramica 164
cerchio di centrocampo 167
cereali 116
cerotto 94, 191, 210
cervo 224
cesoie da giardiniere 65
cespuglio 66
cestino 69, 74
cestino del cucito 166
cestino del pane 122

cesto della bianchieria 61
cetriolo 81
check-in 41
chiatta 44
chiave 110
chiave inglese 110
chiavetta USB 134
chiesa 139
chiocciola 229
chiodi 109
chiropratica 215
chitarra acustica 158
chitarra elettrica 159
ciabatta 89
ciabatte infradito 155
cibo e beverande 103
cibo per animali domestici 222
ciclismo su pista 190
cicogna 227
cicoria ripassata in padella 119
cigno 227
ciliegia 79
cima 182
cinema 147
cinghiale 224
cinta 107
cintura di sicurezza 23
cioccolata 76
cioccolata calda 115
cioccolata da spalmare 116
cipolla 82
cipresso 232
citofono 51
ciuccio 99
clarinetto 158
clavicola 199
coccinella 229
coccodrillo 223
coda 17, 217
cofano 22
COLAZIONE 115
coleottero 228
colino 56
collage 164
collana 108
collant 107
collare 210, 222
collare antipulci 216
collare elisabettiano 216
collina 235
collirio 205
collo 196
collutorio 95, 203
colomba 226
coltello 124

coltello da burro 124
coltello da carne 123
coltello da formaggio 122
coltello da pesce 122
coltello e la forchetta 59
comignolo 59
commissariato 140
comò 60
comodino 61
computer 128
COMUNICAZIONE E L'INFORMATICA 127
concerto 148
conchiglie 155
concorso ippico 190
condominio 45, 47
coniglio 220
cono di traffico 26
contatore 50
contenitore per le lenti a contatto 205
conto 122
contrabbasso 159
coperta 60
coperta da picnic 153
coperta per bambini 213
copricapo 244
corallo 230
corda 171
corda da campeggio 141
cordolo 25
coriandoli 239
cornetto 89, 116
cornetto alla crema 89
coro 160
CORPO 194
corpo 196, 197
corridoio 150
corsia 25
corvo 226
coscia 196
cosmetici 103
costa 236
costole 199
costoletta 87
costoletta di maiale 119
costume 237, 244
costume da bagno 107, 156, 179
cotton fioc 98
cottura 143
couscous 74
cozza 85
cranio 199
cravatta 107

credenza 53, 57
crema antisettica 94
crema per bambini 98
crema per eritema da pannolino 98
crema solare 94, 156
crêpes 126
criceto 220
cricket 189
crostata 89
crostatina alla frutta 120
cruciverba 163
cruscotto 23
cuccetta 37
cucchiaino 59
cucchiaio 59
cucchiaio da dolce 124
cucchiaio da minestra 124
cucchiaio di legno 57
cuccia 222
cuffia 179
cuffie 158
culla di vimini 99
cuscino 53, 61
custodia per gli occhiali 205
cyclette 171

dadi 163
dadi e bulloni 109
DAL DENTISTA 202
DAL DOTTORE 200
DALL'OTTICO 204
dama 163
danza classica 147
deambulatore 207
decorazioni 239
delfino 230
denti 203
dentiera 203
dentifricio 95, 203
dentista 203
deserto 234
direttore d'orchestra 160
disco 186
diserbante 65
dito 195
dito del piede 195
divano 53
Diwali 241
docce 171
doccia 63
docente 131

dolciumi 100
domino 163
dottore 193
dottoressa 193
drone 161
duty free 41
ecografia 213
ecografista 213
edera 233
EDICOLA 100
efemera 229
Eid al-Fitr 241
elefante 225
elicottero 12
emmental 90
enoteca 112
Epifania 243
erbe aromatiche 74
esame della vista 205
escoriazione 204
ESPRESSIONI DI BASE 8, 18, 46, 70, 114, 142, 168, 192, 218, 238
espresso 115
eye liner 96
FACCENDE DI CASA 67
facchino 37, 161
fagiolini 82
fai da te 143
falco 226
falena 229
FAMIGLIA E AMICI 10
fanale anteriore 22
fard 96
fare shopping 143
fare surf 180
faretto 57
farfalla 228
FARMACIA 92
farmacia 193
farmacista 193
fascia 210
fasciatura 94
FAST FOOD 125
fattoria 47
fave 81
felpa 107
femore 199
fenicottero 226
fermata dell'autobus 31
FERRAMENTA 109
ferri da maglia 166
ferro da stiro 67
FERROVIA 35
festa 29
FESTIVITÀ E FESTE 240
festoni 239
fetta biscottata 116
fettina di manzo 119

fiammiferi 153
fico 79
filobus 31
filo del bucato 68
filo interdentale 203
finestra 45, 50
finestrino 22
fioraio 111
fiori 66
fiori di zucca in pastella 118
FIORI, PIANTE E ALBERI 231
fioriera 65
fisarmonica 158
fischietto 173
fitoterapia 214
fiume 235
flauto 159
flebo 207
flute da spumante 59
foca 230
focaccia 89
fondotinta 96
fontana 140
fontina 90
football americano 189
forbici 134
forbici da tessuto 166
forchetta 124
forchetta da dolce 124
foresta 234
formaggio di capra 90
formica 228
fornello da campeggio 153
forno 57
fotocopiatrice 134
FOTOGRAFIA 161
fragola 80
francobollo 101, 138
fratercula 227
frattura 209
freccette 163
freccia 22
freno 33
freno a mano 23
frigo portatile 153
frigorifero con congelatore 57
fringuello 226
fronte 195
frullatore 55
frusta 57
FRUTTA E VERDURA 78
frutta secca 76

frutto della passione 80
fungo 82, 233
fuochi d'artificio 239
furetto 220
gabbia 222
gabbiano 226
gabinetto 63
galleria d'arte 145
gamba 196
gamberetto 85
gambero 85
gambero d'acqua dolce 85
garage 50
gare automobilistiche 190
garofano 231
garza 210
gattaiola 222
gatto 220
geco 223
gelato 120
gengive 203
ghiacciaio 234
ghirlanda 243
giacca 106
giacca da sci 183
giacca di pelle 34
giacca impermeabile 107
giacinto 231
giallo 7
giardinaggio 143
giardini 145
GIARDINO 64
giardino 66
giavellotto 186
giglio 232
ginnastica artistica 189
ginocchio 196
giocare ai videogiochi 143
giocatore di pallacanestro 175
giocattoli 103
GIOCHI 162
gioco da tavolo 163
gioielleria 164
giornale 101
giorna di Ognissanti 241
GIORNI, MESI E STAGIONI 15
giostrina 98
giradischi 158
giraffa 225
girasole 232
girello 99
giubbotto ad alta visibilità 29

giubbotto di salvataggio 44, 180
giudice di linea 177
gocce 94
GOLF 188
golf car 188
gomito 197
gomitolo di lana 166
gomma da cancellare 130
gonna 106
gorgonzola 91
gorilla 225
graffetta 134
grancassa 158
granchio 85, 230
GRANDE MAGAZZINO 102
gratta e vinci 101
grattugia 55
GRAVIDANZA 212
griglia 153
grillo 228
grondaia 50
grotta 234
gru 226
gruccia 60
guancia 195
guanti 108
guanti da boxe 184
guanti da giardinaggio 64
guanti da portiere 173
guanti da sci 183
guanti di gomma 68
guanti di pelle 34
guardalinee 173
guardare i film 143
guardare la TV 143
gufo 227
guida 145
GUIDARE 24
guida turistica 145
guinzaglio 222
hamburger 87, 126
Hanukkah 241
hockey 189
hockey su ghiaccio 189
Holi 241
hot dog 126
iguana 223
illuminazione 103
immersione subacquea 180
impiegata postale 138
impiegato postale 138

inchiostro 165
IN CITTÀ 139
incubatrice 213
indicatore del carburante 23
infermiera 193, 201
infermiere 193, 201
ingessatura 207
insalata mista 120
insalata verde 119
insalatiera 58, 59
INSETTI 228
insetticida 94
insettifugo 94
ipnoterapia 215
ippica 189
ippopotamo 225
isola 236
ISTRUZIONE 129
jeans 106
jogging 143
judo 185
karatè 185
kayak 44
ketchup 74
kettlebell 171
kickboxing 185
kit di pronto soccorso 191, 193
kiwi 79
lago 235
lampada da tavolo 133
lampadina 49
lampone 80
lancio del peso 187
lasagne 147
latte 92
latte in polvere 99
lavagna bianca 131
lavanda 233
lavanderia 140
lavandino 63
lavastoviglie 67
lavatrice 68
lavello 57
LAVORO 12
lente 161
lenti a contatto 205
lenzuola 61
leone 225
lepre 224
LESIONI 208
lettera 138
letti a castello 60
lettiera 222
lettino 99, 201
lettino del dentista 203
lettino da spiaggia 155
lettino da viaggio 99
letto 61

letto d'ospedale 207
lettore carte di credito 72
lettore Blu-ray® 52
lettore DVD 52
lettura 52
libellula 228
libreria 52, 111
libro 100
libro di enigmistica 101
libro di fumetti 100
libro di testo 131
lillà 233
limone 79
livella 110
livido 209
locale 147
locomotiva 37
lombrico 229
lontra 224
losanga 94
lucchetto per bici 33
luce a muro 53
luce anteriore 33
lucertola 223
luci di Natale 243
lumaca 229
luna 230
luna park 148, 244
lungomare 156
lupo 224
MACCHINA 20
macchina 22
macchina da caffè 55
macchina da cucire 166
macchina fotografica compatta 161
macchina fotografica DSLR 161
macchina per la pasta 56
macchinetta fotografica 145
macedonia 116
MACELLAIO 86
macinapepe 58
maglione 106
maiale 221
maionese 75
MALATTIE 211
MAMMIFERI 224
MANGIARE FUORI 121
mango 79
mano 195, 196
manubri 171
manubrio 33
mappa 19, 101
mappa della città 145
marce 33
marciapiede 25

mare 155
margarina 92
margherita 231
marmellata 74, 116
marmellata di agrumi 74
martedì grasso 241
martello 109
martinetto 29
martin pescatore 226
mascara 96
mascarpone 91
mascella 195
maschera 237, 244
maschera a ossigeno 207
maschera da sci 183
massaggio 215
materassino 153
materasso 61
matita 101, 130, 165
matite colorate 130
mattarello 56
mattonelle 110
mazzo di fiori 239
meccanico 29
medaglia 169
medicina 94, 193
medicina tradizionale cinese 215
medico di base 201
meditazione 215
medusa 230
mela 78
melanzana 81
melone 78
mento 195
menù 123
MERCATO 77
merlo 226
merluzzo 83
mestolo 56
metro a nastro 166
metropolitana 37
metropolitana leggera 37
mezzaluna 55
microonde 57
miele 74
millepiedi 228
minibar 151
minibus 31
mirtillo 79
mischia 174
misuratore di pressione sanguigna 201
mobili 103
mocio 68
moda 103
modellismo 164

mollette da bucato 67
molo 43
monete 72
monitor 207
monolocale 47
montagna 235
montatura 205
monumento 145
mora 79
mortadella 87
mosca 140
moschea 140
moto 34
moto d'acqua 179
MOTOCICLETTA 34
motociclismo 190
mousse al cioccolato 120
mozzarella 91
mucca 221
muesli 116
muffole 97
municipio 140
MUOVERSI PER TRAGHETTO E NAVE 42
muschio 233
museo 145
museruola 222
MUSICA 157
musical 148
musicista 160
muta 180
mutande 106
narciso 231
naso 195
NATALE E CAPODANNO 243
natiche 197
navigatore 23
negozio di alimenti naturali 112
negozio di animali 112
negozio di elettronica 111
NEGOZIO DI FORMAGGI 90
negozio di giocattoli 112
negozio di mobili 111
negozio di musica 112
negozio di scarpe 112
negozio di telefoni 112
nero 7
netball 190
night 148
nocca 195

noodles 75
numero di targa 22
nuvole 236
obliteratrice 38
oca 221
occhiali 205
occhiali da sole 156
occhialini 179
occhio 195
olio di oliva 75
olio essenziale 214
olio vegetale 69, 75
olive 76
ombrello 7
ombrellone 155
ombretto 96
omelette 126
omeopatia 214
omero 197
omogeneizzati 98
onde 155
onisco 229
opera 148
ORA E IL PASSAGGIO DEL TEMPO 14
orario 11
orata 84
orata alla griglia 119
orca marina 230
orchestra 160
orchidea 232
orecchini 108
orecchio 195
orefice 112
ormeggio 44
orpello 243
orso 225
OSPEDALE 206
ospedale 140, 193
ostacoli 186
osteopatia 215
ostetrica 213
ostrica 85
ottico 112, 205
ovatta 98
pacco 138
paddle 180
padella 55
pagaia 180
pagliaccetto 97
pala 17
paletta da giardiniere 65
paletta per la spazzatura 68
pali di porta 174
PALLACANESTRO 175
pallina natalizia 242
partita di pallacanestro 175
palla da ginnastica 171

palla da pallacanestro 175
pallamano 189
pallanuoto 190
pallavolo 190
pallina da golf 188
pallina da squash 176
pallina da tennis 177
pallone da calcio 173
pallone da rugby 174
pallone da spiaggia 155
palmo 195
palude 235
panca 171
pancetta 87
pane 69
PANETTERIA E PASTICCERIA 88
panettone 89
panini 88, 116, 126
panna 92
panna cotta 120
pannolino 98, 213
pantacollant 106
pantaloni 107
pantofole 108
papavero 232
pappagallino ondulato 220
pappagallo 217
pappagallo 220
parabrezza 22
paradenti 184
paramedico 193
parasole 65
parastinchi 173
paratesta 184
paraurti 22
paravento 155
parcheggio 24, 25
parcheggio accessibile 24
parchimetro 25
parco 140
parco giochi 140
PARLA DI TE 9
parmigiano 91
parrucchiere 112
partita di calcio 172
Pasqua 241
Pasqua ebraica 241
passaggio a livello 25
passaporto 41
passeggino 99
passerella 43
passero 227
pasta 75, 118
pastelli 165
pastiglia 94, 191

PASTI PRINCIPALI 117
patata 82
patate arrosto 120
patatine fritte 76, 119, 126
patio 66
pattinaggio su ghiaccio 182
pattini da ghiaccio 182
pattumiera a pedale 54
pavimento in legno 64
pavone 227
paziente 193
pecora 221
pecorino 91
pedale 33
pelapatate 56
pellicano 227
pellicola 54
penisola 236
penna 101, 132, 165
pennello 110, 165
pentola 56
pepe 75
peperoncino 81
peperone rosso 82
pera 80
perforatrice 133
perone 199
pesca 80, 189
pescanoce 79
pesciolino rosso 220
PESCIVENDOLO 83
pettine 110
pettirosso 227
petto di pollo 87
piano cottura 57
pianoforte 159
pianta 195
piastrelle 57
piatti 159
piattino 113, 124
piatto 59
piatto da portata 58
piatto fondo 124
piatto misto di mare 118
piatto piano 124
picchetto da tenda 141
piccione 227
piccozza da ghiaccio 182
piede 195, 196
pigiama 106
pilota 41
ping pong 190
pinguino 227
pinne 156, 179

pino 233
pinze 110
pinzette 210
pioppo 233
piscina 179
piselli 82
pista 41, 183
pista da corsa 187
pittura a olio 165
pittura facciale 244
piuma 237
piumone 61
pizza 126
pizzicheria 111
platano 233
pneumatico 22, 33
podio 169
poggiapiedi 53
poggiatesta 23
polipo 85
pollice 195
pollo 221
pollo al forno 119
polpaccio 197
polpette al sugo 119
polso 195
poltrona 53, 61
pomata 210
pomodoro 82
pompa di benzina 25
pompa per bicicletta 33
pompelmo 79
ponte 24
pony 220
popcorn 76
porcellino d'India 220
porchetta 87
porro 82
porta 167, 173
portabagagli 22
PORTA D'INGRESSO 51
porta d'ingresso 50
portapane 54
portasciugamani 63
portatile 133
porta TV 53
porte scorrevoli 38
porticciolo 44
portiera 22
portiere 173
porto 43
Post-it® 134
prateria 234
prato 66
presepio 243
preservativo 94
primula 232
PROBLEMI CON LA MACCHINA 27

PRODOTTI FRESCHI E
LATTICINI 92
PRODOTTI PER
BAMBINI 97
profiteroles 120
prolunga 49
pronto soccorso 206
prosciutto 87
provolone 91
prua 17
pullman 31
punti 207
punto di pedaggio 26
puntura 209
putter 188
puzzle 163
quaderno 130
quadro 53
quadro elettrico 49
quercia 233
raccattapalle 177
racchetta da
badminton 176
racchetta da
squash 176
racchetta da
tennis 177
raccoglitore ad
anelli 130
radicchio 82
radio 52, 199
radiografia 207
radiosveglia 60
ragno 229
Ramadan 241
ramponi 182
rana 223
ranuncolo 231
rasoio 95
rastrello 64
ratto 220
reception 151
receptionist 151
recipiente
graduato 56
regalo 239
reggiseno 105
remi 180
reparto 207
ribes rosso 80
ricamo 164
riccio 85, 224, 230
ricevuta 72
ricotta 91
riflessologia 215
righello 131
rilevatore di fumo 50
ring 184
rinoceronte 225
ripiano 57
ripiano portabagagli
37

riso 75
risotto 118
ristagno d'acqua tra
le rocce 236
ristorante 148
ritiro bagagli 40
rivista 101
rocce 235
rollè 119
rosa 232
rospo 223
rossetto 96
rosso 7
rotolo di carta
igienica 63
rotonda 26
rotore 17
rotula 199
router senza fili 128
rubinetto 57, 63
rugbista 174
RUGBY 174
rugby 174
rullo per verniciare
110
ruota 22, 33
ruota di scorta 29
ruscello 235
sabbia 155
sacco a pelo 153
sacco da boxe 184
sacco della
spazzatura 54
SALA DA PRANZO 58
sala d'attesa 201
salamandra 223
salame 87
sala operatoria 207
sala parto 213
sale 75
sale e pepe 123
salice 233
salmone 84
salmone affumicato
118
salone di bellezza
111
salopette 183
SALOTTO 52
salotto 53
salsiccia 87
salsiera 58
saltimbocca 119
salto con l'asta 187
salto in alto 186
salto in lungo 186
salvagente 43
salviette umidificate
98
sandali 108
sapone 62, 95

sardina 84
sassofono 159
scacchi 163
scaffale 53
scala a libretto 110
scalpello 109
scamorza 91
scanner 134
scarafaggio 228
scarpe da boxe 184
scarpe da ginnastica
108
scarpe da
pallacanestro 175
scarpe stringate 108
scarpette chiodate
187
scarpine 97
scarpini da calcio 173
scarponi da sci 183
scarponi da
snowboard 183
scatola 138
scatola di cioccolatini
239
schedario 133
scheda SD 161
scheggia 209
SCHELETRO 198
scheletro 199
scherma 185
schermo doccia 63
schiacciapatate 56
schiena 197
schiuma da barba 95
sci 183
sciarpa 108
sci d'acqua 180
scimmia 225
scimpanzé 225
sciroppo per la tosse
94
scodella 56
scogliera 236
scoiattolo 224
scolapasta 55
scolapiatti 57
scopa 67
scopino del water 63
scotch® 134
scottatura 209
scrivania 133
sdraio 155
secchiello e la
paletta 155
secchio 67
sedano 81
sedia 122
sedia a rotelle 207
sedia dell'arbitro 177
sedia girevole 134
sedia pieghevole 153

sedile per bambini
99
sega 110
seggiolone 99
segnalini 163
sellino 33
semaforo 26
semifreddo 120
sentiero 66
serpente 223
serra 64
serranda 50
SERATE FUORI 146
sfilata 244
sgombro 84
shampoo 95
sigaretta 100
sigaro 100
SIM 128
sinagoga 140
siringa 191, 201
sistema SoundBar
158
skateboard 190
slitta 182
smalto per le unghie
96
smartphone 128
snooker 190
snorkelling 180
snowboard 183
sogliola 84
sole 236
sollevamento pesi
190
soprammobile 53
spalla 197
spartito 160
spatola 56
spazzola per capelli
96
spazzolino da denti
95, 203
specchietto laterale
22
specchietto
retrovisore 23
specchio 61, 63
spettacolo comico
147
spettatori 169
spezie 75
SPIAGGIA 154
spigola 84
spilla da balia 166
spillatrice 134
spilli 166
spinaci 82
spinaci all'agro 120
spina dorsale 199
spogliatoio 171
sport 143

SPORT ACQUATICI 178
SPORT DA
COMBATTIMENTO
184
SPORT DI RACCHETTA
176
sportello
bancomat 136
SPORT INVERNALI 181
sportiva 169
sportivo 169
spray per capelli 96
spugna 63, 68
spugna per la doccia
62
spumante 239
squadra sportiva 169
squalo 230
squash 175
stadio 169
staffetta 187
stagno 235
stalla 222
stampante 134
stampelle 206
STANZA DA LETTO 60
stanza di letto 61
stazione ferroviaria
38
steccato 66
stella marina 230
stelle 236
stelle filanti 239
stendino 67
sterno 199
stetoscopio 201
stivali 34, 108
stivali di gomma 65
straccio 67
strada 26
strisce pedonali 26
strofinaccio 68
struzzo 227
studente 131
studentessa 131
stufa 49
stufa a legna 50
stuzzicadenti 123
succo d'arancia 115
succo di frutta 76
superalcolici 76
SUPERMERCATO 73
sushi 126
susina 80
tabacco 101
tabella di
misurazione della
vista 205
tabellone delle
partenze 37, 41
tabellone segnapunti
169

tablet 128
tacchi alti 108
tacchino 221
taccuino 101, 133
tachimetro 23
taekwondo 185
tagliaerba 65
tagliere 55
taglio 209
tai chi 185
talassoterapia 215
taleggio 91
tallone 195
talpa 224
tamburo rullante 159
tapis roulant 171
tappetino da bagno 62
tappeto 53, 61
tartaruga 223
tartaruga acquatica 223
tasso 224
tasso di cambio 136
tastiera 159
tavola da stiro 68
tavola da surf 180
tavolino 53
tavolo 123
tavolozza 165
tazza 113
tazza e il piattino 59
tè 115
teatro 148
tee 188
teglia 55
tela 165
telaio 33
telecomando 52
telefono 134
telefono
    d'emergenza 29

televisore 53
telone esterno 141
telone
    impermeabile 141
temperamatite 131
TEMPO 16
tenda 141, 153
tenda veneziana 53
tende 52, 61
tennis 177
tennista 177
TERAPIE ALTERNATIVE 214
tergicristallo 22
termometro 201
termosifone 50
termostato 50
terra 96
TERRA, MARE E CIELO 234
terreno agricolo 234
tessera magnetica 151
tessuti d'arredo 103
tessuto 166
test di gravidanza 213
testa 196
tetto 45, 50
tettuccio 22
tibia 196, 199
tigre 225
timpano 196
tiramisù 120
tiro al bersaglio 190
tiro con l'arco 189
toast 126
tocco di carne 87
tonno 84
topo 224
torace 196
torcia 153

tordo 227
tornello 38
toro 221
torta 89, 239
torta della nonna 120
torta di mele 120
tortellini 118
tostapane 56
tovaglia 123
tovagliolo 58, 124
traghetto 44
traliccio 66
tram 31
trampolino 179
transatlantico 44
trapano da dentista 203
trapano elettrico 109
trapunta 61
trasportino per
    animali domestici 216
TRASPORTO AEREO 39
treno 38
treppiede 161
triangolo di
    segnalazione 29
tribunale 139
tribune 169
tric-trac 163
tritone 223
trofeo 169
tromba 159
trombone 159
tronchetto di
    Natale 243
trota 84
T-shirt 107
tuba 160
tubo da giardino 64
tubo di scarico 50
tubo orizzontale 33

tulipano 232
tunnel 26
tuta da ginnastica 171
tuta da sci 183
tutina 97, 213
UCCELLI 226
uffici 140
UFFICIO 132
ufficio di cambio 136
UFFICIO POSTALE 137
ufficio turistico 145
ulivo 233
ulna 199
uncinetto 166
unghia 195
unghia del piede 195
uovo 92
utensili da cucina 103
uva 79
vagone ristorante 37
valigia 41
vallata 235
vanga 65
vano portaoggetti 23
vasca da bagno 63
vaschetta per il
    bagnetto 99
vaschetta porta-
    corrispondenza 133
vaso 65
vaso per fiori 66
vellutata 118
ventilatore da
    soffitto 49
verde 7
vernice 109
vertebre 199
vescica 209
vespa 229

vestaglia 106
VESTITI E SCARPE 104
veterinario 216
viaggio 143
viale 50
videocamera con
    casco 34
villino 47
vino 76
viola 232
violetta 232
violino 160
violoncello 158
vischio 243
VISITE TURISTICHE 144
viso 195, 195
vite 233
vitello tonnato 119
viti 110
vivaio 111
vogatore 171
volano 176
volante 23
volpe 224
vongola 85
vulcano 235
windsurf 180
wok 57
wrestling 185
xilofono 160
yacht 44
yogurt 92
zaino 131
zanzara 229
zappa 65
zucca 82
zucchero 75
zucchero a velo 74
zucchina 81
zuppa 118
zuppa di pesce 118

PHOTO CREDITS